TOWARDS SELF-MEANING

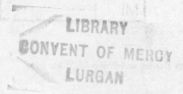
Garrett Barden and
Philip McShane S.J.

GILL AND MACMILLAN   DUBLIN

First published in 1969
Gill and Macmillan Limited
2 Belvedere Place
Dublin 1.

© Garett Barden and Philip McShane 1909

Cover design by Des Fitzgerald

SBN 7171 0230 0 Paper Bound Edition
SBN 7171 0231 9 Case Bound Edition

Printed and bound in the Republic of Ireland
by Hely Thom Limited, Dublin.

to

Angela

ACKNOWLEDGEMENTS

The publishers wish to thank the following for permission to include copyright material in this book:
MacGibbon and Kee for 'Ascetic' and 'I may reap' by Patrick Kavanagh.

CONTENTS

in the end

may find

nething not sold for a penny

in the slums of Mind.

That I may break
  With these hands
The bread of wisdom that grows
  In the other lands.

For this, for this
  Do I wear
The rags of hunger and climb
  The unending stair.

Patrick Kavanagh's *Ascetic*

Preface

THIS little book was written in a winter of preoccupations for both authors, but the idea of writing it originated several years ago in our mutual struggle towards self-meaning as mediated by the works of Fr Lonergan. It was written thus, despite pre-occupations, to meet an evident and immediate need in this area. Our intention was not to present a complete coherent account of Fr Lonergan's approach to philosophy, but to introduce it. The specialist will find our introduction inadequate and incomplete, but there is a strategy in the inadequacy and in the incompleteness. A central element in that strategy is the avoidance of the tendency of decadence to summarize rather than expand the expression of the original thinker's thought. Serious work with this short unscientific book should bring the reader to appreciate the basic lacunae in it and lead him or her still further to the works of Fr Lonergan for more adequate and scientific expression of the notion of being, of substance, of structured objectivity, of canons of method, of genuineness etc.

We would like to thank Fr Conn O'Donovan S.J. of Milltown Park, Dublin, both for helpful suggestions and for continual encouragement. Our thanks are due also to Miss Angela Kirby for a like encouragement as well as for typing assistance: by the time of the appearance of this book she will have been happily married by both of us.

Philip McShane
Garrett Barden
Spring, 1968

TOWARDS SELF-MEANING

Introduction

'THE high daring of self-reflection, that precondition of all truthfulness, has degenerated along the path of ideological theory.'[1]

If you are trying to teach someone how to drive a car there comes a point when you have to vacate the driving seat and let the learner take your place. Eventually the learner has to teach himself. Certainly he can profit from the hints that the experienced driver gives him, but in the end he must drive himself. This book is something like the hints the experienced driver can give.

This is neither a long nor, at first glance, a difficult book. You can read it in a couple of hours and in that time you will gain a little information. You will become familiar with words and phrases, and with some of the main points to which we return again and again. But unless you have already seriously ventured into the field of scientific self-attention, most likely you will have missed the point.

This is not a difficult book in that almost no specialist knowledge is required of the reader. You do not have to be a mathematician, a physicist, a sociologist, an artist, or a philosopher to read this book. It is true that a certain amount of mathematics may tax the reader's energy, but at no point do we assume a specialist's background of knowledge.

And yet in a more important sense it is a difficult book. It is difficult because what we ask you to do is both difficult and rare. What we are asking is something akin to Karl Jaspers's 'high daring of self-reflection'.

Very probably the term 'self-reflection' is not meaningless to you. Yet if you push yourself a little you may find your ideas on the precise nature of that activity are obscure. Images of the hermit meditating in his cell, the Buddhist monk reaching out towards enlightenment, the philosopher struggling out of the

[1]Karl Jaspers, *The Origin and Goal of History*, London 1953, 132.

cave of Plato's parable, Descartes beside his stove, or Kant in his study in Koenigsberg, come to mind. These images are not wrong; they give you what we shall later explain as a symbolic appreciation of the activity named 'self-reflection'. But perhaps you would be somewhat at a loss if you were asked to undertake this self-reflection. Our book is concerned with self-reflection and self-meaning. It is a series of hints on how to perform this personal and long-term experiment.

Our title, 'Self-Meaning', is ambiguous. Deliberately so. Although as you progress in the book the dimensions and scope of the title will become clearer, still it is probably worth while to give a preliminary suggestion of these dimensions.

Think for a moment of some of the ways in which you use the term 'meaning'. If you come across some unfamiliar writing which you are unable to read, you say, What does it mean? People often ask about the meaning of a painting or perhaps a film or play. In detective stories the detective asks about the meaning of a clue. Consider phrases like; What I mean is, I shall explain what I mean, My meaning is quite plain. The term 'meaning' is both a noun and the present participle of the verb 'to mean'.

Self-meaning, then, will be a twofold effort. First it will be the personal effort to come to terms with yourself. It will be the effort to discover what kind of a thing you are. It will be an effort to answer the question, What is a man? If you consider that question a moment, another difficulty will surely strike you. The science of medicine tries to discover what a man is and we are not doing medical research in this book. Human biology, psychology, sociology and so on are all trying to answer that question and yet we are not undertaking research in any of these subjects. Here we are faced with the first and basic peculiarity of this science. We are attempting to understand our own knowing, we are trying to discover what happens when we know.

Understanding is one of the operations that occur in any instance of human knowing and so it can be taken as an example. The significance of the example will become clearer as the book proceeds. Sometimes you are faced with a problem and cannot find the solution. You do not understand. You stare at the problem for a time, you rack your brains, and then suddenly you've got it. Have you ever seen someone struggling with a problem? His face is often tense and his whole body seems to bear down on the problem, then suddenly he explodes into happiness, he relaxes and smiles. The problem is solved. What is important to note here though, is that beneath the bodily expressions of tension and glee some activity is going on which is not accessible directly to you. You presume that he is asking questions, that he has come to a solution, because that is what you do when you are faced with a problem. How do you know that you ask questions and come to a solution? Did someone have to tell you? Or did you experience yourself asking questions and coming to solutions? Surely you experience yourself trying to solve problems. Our first movement in the approach to self-meaning is then the attempt to reflect on this experience of solving problems, this experience of asking questions, of racking your brains, of suddenly getting it, of checking your solution to see if it fits all the evidence and so on.

That may seem like quite a simple programme. In fact it is not. As Aquinas said, it requires a diligent and subtle investigation. But it is an investigation which is ineluctably personal. Either you do it yourself or you don't do it. No one else can do it for you. This book cannot do it for you. Like the driving teacher we can give hints, but like the learner you have to drive eventually yourself. For this reason, if you read it properly, this is a difficult book.

Because the investigation is personal we do not ask you to believe anything we say here. Belief is a perfectly reasonable activity, as we show later. But its place is not here. It is of course possible to believe what we write. It is perfectly possible to take a sentence or several sentences and decide to believe them on our word. But we are not asking you to do this. We are asking you to perform an experiment. We are asking you to attempt the high daring of self-reflection.

As you proceed in the experiment, as you introspectively study your conscious activities of experiencing, enquiring, understanding, judging, you will discover not only the acts but also the subject. You will find the subject who means. And this is the second movement. You will discover yourself as the source of inquiry and understanding and judging. You will discover yourself as the meaning subject. At this point, obscurely at first, but with developing clarity, the 'high daring' of the experiment will be revealed. For the discovery of yourself as meaning subject illuminates in a single beam both the responsibility and the possibilities of the subject.

The discovery of the subject as central source of meaning provides us with a new way into the analysis of subjectivity, and the personal responsibility of the judging subject comes to the fore. For, the discovery of the subject as source of meaning does not throw overboard the notion of truth, but that notion is refined, an inadequate and incorrect theory of objectivity is rejected, and a more refined and accurate theory developed. Further, the subject is not merely a knowing subject but also a subject who chooses and implements. For this reason this effort at self-meaning is shown to be related both to sociological and to political theory.

The notion of the possibilities of the subject throws some light on another aspect of self-meaning. For there are more possibilities than are actually realized. The subject at any one instant could become a number of things, but in fact he becomes only one thing. Out of the many possible results, only one is realized. The range of possibilities at any given time is the range of the person's effective liberty; he can become any of the possibilities but he cannot become what is not possible. Notice also that this range of possibilities is associated with the person's understanding of himself. The subject is, then, reponsible for becoming what he turns out to be. This notion is familiar from contemporary existentialist writings. We have come to this position in a different way perhaps, and this mode of reaching the conclusion places the conclusion in a slightly different perspective. For many existential thinkers, who have currently abandoned an inadequate theory of objectivity, have not yet discovered an adequate theory and so are at times left in the curious position of denying expressly what they in fact affirm implicitly.

Not only are many possibilities open to the subject, but he must select. How is he to select correctly? Or are we here in the sphere of the arbitrary? Or are we perhaps to remain within the bounds of tradition, since tradition often points out which of the many possibilities is to be chosen? Still, it does not seem that tradition is in the final analysis an adequate reason for making one choice rather than another. For traditions, like any other human product, can be decadent, and following a decadent tradition is hardly the ideal. Again, to be realistic in the contemporary world, we would have to ask which tradition to follow, for we are faced now not with one tradition but with several conflicting traditions. We might follow the tradition we were born into, but where is the guarantee that it is the correct one? Once more the subject is thrown back on himself, on his own responsibility. Accordingly, he must become a critical subject.

But how is one to become a critical subject? It is tempting to look for the pat answer. Brought up in a society where instant information is highly regarded and ignorance or uncertainty thought to be the sign of either stupidity or laziness, we are inclined to turn to anyone who will offer a slick reply. If one authority is discredited, we turn to another as the winds of fashion dictate. But to seek the pat answer is to abandon intelligence; it is in fact to say that to be a man is too difficult. And so we are led to another theme that runs through our book: authentic nescience. To be a critical subject is not to be infallible. Primarily being a critical subject means having a grasp of the structure of your knowing and doing, and from this base working out to a discovery of what you know and what you believe and what you don't know, of what you really understand and what you have a verbal familiarity with. Primarily it means being critical of yourself. Nor is it achieved in a year or several years. We have found after several years, and each of us in his own time and in slightly different ways, that as we advanced and at times perhaps thought we were getting there, new dimensions opened out to reveal further unthought-of possibilities.

Self-meaning indicates the development of the person. If we have concentrated in the Introduction on theoretic meaning, still we have vaguely indicated other non-theoretic modes. Besides science there is art, and here too is a manner of meaning. Self-meaning, then, will not ignore this aspect of human living, and, indeed, development in self-meaning, as it is concomitant with developing understanding in science and common sense, goes with development in artistic appreciation also. For if the subject is source, he is also centre of meaning, and the meeting place of science and art is neither book, nor course, nor college, but the meaning subject. It is the same subject who enquires, understands, solves problems, appreciates music, looks at a painting, or writes a poem.

Self-meaning, since it illuminates both the freedom and the responsibility of the subject, because it reveals the free and responsible subject, is in the last analysis a conversion. As the book progresses the nature of this conversion will gradually be revealed. Like everything else about our experiment this conversion will be personal, it will be something that no other human can do for you. Slowly, however, another dimension of its personal character will be discovered. For it is a conversion not merely of a person, but to Three Persons, and at this point authentic nescience becomes a mystery.

So much then for a description of the journey. It is time to begin.

1

Horizons

WE may begin with the story of the lady who invited the physicist to tea. As the meal drew to a close, the lady remarked that she had always wanted to understand Einstein's Theory of Relativity, and since she now had a real physicist to talk to, perhaps he could explain it to her? 'Of course I don't know any physics and I always hated mathematics, so you would have to avoid all that terminology and the use of formulae. But I know you are an excellent physicist and you surely will be able to explain it to me, in my own simple words.' The point of the story is clear—the lady has no conception of what understanding Einstein's theory involves. That the physicist spent years studying before he came to have some understanding of it means little to her. Her horizon is the limited horizon of common sense. Her reaction to what lies outside that horizon may be the extreme one which claims that what is outside her horizon just isn't, or the less extreme one that acknowledges a 'beyond' but would hope that whatever is of value 'beyond' would surely be capable of contraction to within her horizon.

One might represent diagramatically the various horizons as concentric circles, the horizon of common sense fitting within the horizon of science. Now we ask the reader to draw yet another outside circle to represent the horizon of methodology.

It is more than likely that the reader will find it hard to accept or envisage such a horizon but we hope to bring him to intelligently accept and vaguely envisage it. Is that hope vain? Certainly one should not expect too much. After all, if our claim is correct, our efforts here are rather akin to the efforts of the physicist to explain Einstein to the lady. Still the attempt has its value. First of all, there are those who have already come in contact with the work of Bernard Lonergan and suspect that it is worth more attention. This short book can serve as an encouragement and an initiation. Secondly, our times are times of popularization. Popularization, when it is not recognized as such, can be harmful to science, especially to such a science as theology. But when popularization is undertaken and accepted as such, then it is worthwhile. For while it does not lead the reader genuinely to share the relevant scientific horizon—unless he is prepared to follow up the popular introduction—still it can create a climate of tolerance for the science and its pursuit.

The science in question is that of introspective methodology. That there is such a science is something we must gradually substantiate. Just as the common-sense attitude does not easily acknowledge the scientific horizon, so neither common sense nor science can easily acknowledge this further methodological horizon. Thus the biologist's reaction to our claim that part of introspective methodology deals with the method of biology may be to say, 'But surely I'm the man to deal with that: I have been doing biology for years and am extremely familiar with its method'. And to convince him that familiarity with the method of biology is a far cry from the understanding of it given by methodology or metabiology is no easy task.

One way of leading the scientist, or the common sense person, to some appreciation of the existence and nature of this science of methodology is to indicate the various problems of method that are present in contemporary culture. The difficulty of such indications, however, is that they can be appreciated only by the person engaged in the relevant field. Thus, there are basic methodological problems in contemporary physics, particularly in quantum mechanics and relativity, but for any reader who is not actually engaged in these fields, the existence of such problems will be a matter of belief. And even the quantum physicist may puzzle over our use of the expression 'methodological problems'. He will grant that there is obscurity about the relation of quantum theory to reality or about indeterminacy: but why 'methodological'?

One may say that a problem of method is a problem of know-how or know-what-we're-doing. Putting the problem this way helps to throw the stress where it should be: on the person doing the science and not on the science conceived of in some strange way as independent of mind. Now from this angle the problem in quantum theory would be expressed as 'What-are-we-at in doing quantum mechanics?' To elaborate on that problem would be out of place here and meaningless for the ordinary reader: it is for the interested specialist to follow up the lead and re-express his problems in this mode.

One might note such problems of know-how in the various knowings and doings of contemporary culture, from the foundations of mathematics and logic to psychology and sociology, from the field of aesthetics and literary criticism to basic questions regarding liturgy. But let us restrict ourselves here to noting the methodological problems within the field of theology: there the problems are both of more general interest and more evident and crucial. Do we know-what-we're-doing when we're doing theology, do we know-how to go about it? Ask a theologian! Is theology a science at all, or is it just refined common sense? Is it tied to a particular culture, or is it catholic, universal? Is it familiarity with the Bible, or is it understanding the Apostles' Creed? There may be common consent that it is faith seeking understanding but what do we mean by understanding? And this last question brings us close to the focus of both the problem and its solution.

What is understanding? It may be briefly described as what is rare in the stupid and what occurs more frequently in the intelligent. But can we get beyond this description? Consider more closely the What-question, What is understanding? Let us compare it to other such questions, as What is a dog? What is light? These questions too can be answered descriptively and acceptably: the dog can be described in terms of evident shape and activities; light can be described in terms of colour. But besides these descriptions there are sciences which deal with dogs and light. In them dogs and light are taken as data to be understood, and the understanding required constitutes respectively the sciences of animal psychology and physics. Comparing this with our question What is understanding?, the possibility of a parallel should not be too unacceptable. Our datum in this case is understanding, our own understanding. Just as the biologist has experience of dogs so we have experience of our own acts of understanding. Just as the biologist can centre his attention on that experience of dogs, familiarize himself with all sorts of specimens and slowly grow in an understanding of animals and plants, so we may centre our attention on our own acts of understanding, accumulate specimens from various fields, and slowly grow in an understanding of our understanding. There are of course professional philosophers who would deny that we could attend to ourselves and grow in an understanding of our understanding. But how do they reach this conclusion: by not attending to themselves, by not trying to understand themselves?

Again, while authority is not a popular source of proof, it is nice to know that great men are on our side. Neither Aquinas nor Aristotle had any doubts as to how to go about understanding the nature of intelligence: ' . . . The species therefore of the thing actually understood is the species of the understanding itself; hence it is that understanding can understand itself through this species. Thus the philosopher in an earlier passage studied the nature of possible intellect by studying the very act of understanding and the object that is understood'.[1] One might recall too the Socratic stress on self-knowledge, Augustine's stress on introspection, Descartes's quest for method, and Kant's search for a science that should determine *a priori* the possibilities, principles, and extent of human knowledge.[2] In each there is an appreciation of, and a groping towards, knowledge of knowledge. Nearer our own times we have a tradition of interest in the existential subject running from Kierkegaard to Heidegger, but that interest never blossomed out into a genuine science of the subject. At the end of his big book on Heidegger, W. J. Richardson poses various questions and concludes, 'But these are questions, questions, questions. Are there no answers to be had? What must we do to find them?'[3] While Richardson answers that last question with a quotation from Heidegger, 'We must do nothing but wait', we prefer to recommend the introspective technique by which the subject, the reader, would get to grips with himself in a novel and fundamental way. This getting to grips with oneself is no mean task, and there is the ever present danger of abandoning it in favour of a mastery of the language of the new science. 'As you know, mankind has an instinctive antipathy to intellectual novelties; one of the ways in which this shows itself is that any such novelty is immediately reduced to its very smallest compass, and if possible embodied in some catch-word.'[4] For this reason we will be at pains throughout to keep the reader from the illusion that we are making a methodologist out of him or her.

[1] From St Thomas's commentary on Aristotle, *In III De Anima*, lect. 9, n. 724.

[2] *Critique of Pure Reason*, Introduction, section 3.

[3] *Heidegger: Through Phenomenology to Thought*. The Hague 1963, 641.

[4] S. Freud, *General Introduction to Psychoanalysis*, Perma Books, New York 1953, 225.

We offer only signposts, elementary directions, a grammar of procedure. We have both been struggling with the science of introspective methodology for years now. Its fruits are as slow in coming forth as they are fundamental and significant personally and culturally. These fruits of self-understanding can only be vaguely indicated in one short book. 'Anyone who has worked a while at "Spiritual Exercises" will know how difficult is the examination of conscience, how elusive the determination of motives, how alien to nature the effort to explore the inner life of the soul. Most of us would hardly undertake such exercises except on the very best authority in the spiritual life, yet, having done so, would probably agree that the experiment was profitable. Should we expect the appropriation of cognitional process to be much easier than that of motives, or the former to be any less profitable philosophically than the latter is ascetically? The suggestion is that, if Lonergan really has something to offer intellectually, and urges self-appropriation as the one adequate route to the goal, then it seems unreasonable to expect to reach it at the end of reading a book or an article.'[5]

The effort to understand one's own knowing can be immediately related to the history of philosophy, to the quest for wisdom which was focused by Aristotle. Every science has its history, its period of confusion and myth, its eventual emergence as a definite science. Before chemistry, there was alchemy, before astronomy there was astrology. So in philosophy. There is clear evidence that Aristotle, Augustine and Aquinas all indulged in introspective understanding, but none of them elevated it into a scientific technique. If we are correct, that elevation is demanded by, and being realized in, our own times. If we are correct, then the establishment of introspective technique marks a transition in philosophy analogous to the transition from alchemy to chemistry. The relation between introspective understanding and the results of such men as

[5] F. E. Crowe, 'The Exigent Mind', *Continuum,* 1964, 328.

Aristotle will obviously not be clear to the reader from what we have said. And indeed we may remark that even if it were spelled out, the view proposed would hardly find wide acceptance: an essential transition in a science is always incredible to those long familiar with a prior stage, a prior view. As Max Planck put it, a new scientific position does not gain general acceptance by making opponents change their minds—it does so by holding its own until old age has retired them from their professional chairs.[6]

Again one may see this transition on the broader canvas of history. Karl Jaspers[7] places a basic axis of history in the period between 800 and 200 B.C. when man in some way came of age in Greece, in Persia, in Israel, in India, in China.[8] Later in the context of a discussion of contemporary culture he points to the needs of the contemporary scene and to the possibility of a new axis.[9] Might we suggest that there is something axial about the emergence of introspective methodology as a scientific technique?

What are the fruits of that emergence? Two aspects immediately suggest themselves, one negative, the other positive. The negative aspect is not unrelated to Jaspers's reflection: 'Wonder at the mystery is itself a fruitful act of understanding in that it affords a point of departure for further research. It may even be the goal of all understanding, since it means penetrating through the greatest possible amount of knowledge to authentic nescience, instead of allowing Being to disappear by absolutizing it away into a self-enclosed object of cognition'.[10] The negative aspect is the reaching of authentic nescience. It is a common human failing to mistake eloquence for explanation

[6]M. Planck, *Scientific Autobiography and Other Papers,* edited by F. Gaynor, New York 1949, 33ff.
[7]K. Jaspers, *The Origin and Goal of History,* London 1953.
[8]*Op. cit.,* Chapter 1.
[9]*Op. cit.,* 97
[10]*Op. cit.,* 18

and familiarity for understanding. Socrates' criticism was an effort to reveal to the Greeks that in a peculiar way they didn't know what they were talking about. Introspective understanding opens up the possibility of the reader's appreciating his own nescience within a new horizon. Such an appreciation is of enormous significance in our times when common sense is so meshed with common nonsense, when the human sciences and theology are bandied about in popular parlance. And here we may move to the positive aspects of the fruit of methodology: for, introspective methodology offers man the possibility of getting to grips with his meaning at its focus. Existentialism and historical consciousness have succeeded in underlining man's creativity of his own essence. That emergent essence is centrally on the level of mind, and the more man appreciates the nature of the emergence of meaning, the more adequately will he contribute creatively to that emergence. That appreciation will enable him to move from a state of spontaneous use of his intelligence in his doing to a level of intelligent guidance of that use.[11] But these are difficult matters with which we will not deal in this short book. We may add however a final word on the concrete factual nature of introspective methodology and on its relation to theology.

As we shall see clearly in the following chapters, methodology is not an abstract deductive science: it moves from the experience of knowing and doing to an understanding of that knowing and doing. The knowing and doing is concerned with the concrete and a significant part of it is the range of empirical human sciences. Now since the only correct general form of the understanding of man as he is is theological, we can see that some meshing of theology, methodology, and the human sciences is involved. The conclusion of an introduction to an introductory book on methodology is no place to tackle such an enormous

[11]Cf. B. Lonergan, *De Deo Trino, Pars Systematica*, Rome 1964, Q. XXI, 'Quaenam sit analogia subjecti temporalis et subjecti aeterni'.

issue. But a few pointers may be given. First, then, it is to be noted that what the human sciences have in common is not first principles or propositions but method. Secondly, there is the old tag regarding faith illuminating reason. Now reason's processes are the concern of methodology, and so one may expect an illumination of method by faith. That illumination can occur within theology, and it is primarily through the illumination of method by faith that theology must exercise her traditional queenly role. That all this puts a demand on the contemporary theologian to cross the horizon of introspective methodology should be evident.

We may conclude with a quotation which indicates a further context of our work, brings together much that we have been saying, and serves to acknowledge its source:

> Evidently the question of a Christian Philosophy is not dead. Nor will it die, for in substance it asks how a Catholic can attempt total reflection on man's situation. But it will do no harm to recall that the twelfth century was steeped in Augustine, yet baffled by problems in method and concept-formation that were solved only in the thirteenth by the systematic and ontological distinction between the orders of Grace and Nature. Further, this distinction is stretched to a separation of philosophy and theology, only when there intervenes a further methodological component, namely, that the one valid scientific ideal is an abstract deductivism. Thirdly, against that ideal much contemporary thought, correctly, I believe, is in revolt; but to refute effectively, one must replace, and the replacement must be better than a contrary exaggeration. So I am led to suggest that the issue, which goes by the name of a Christian philosophy, is basically a question on the deepest level of methodology, the one that investigates the operative intellectual ideals not only of scientists and philosophers but also, since Catholic truth is involved, theologians. It is I fear, in Vico's phrase, a *scienza nuova*.[12]

[12]B. Lonergan, *Gregorianum* (40), 1959, 182-3, in a review.

2

Pillars of Wisdom

"I WOULD advise none to read this work, unless such as are able and willing to meditate with me in earnest, to detach their minds from commerce with the senses, and likewise to deliver themselves from all injustice.'[1]

We could make Descartes's sentiments entirely ours were it not for the fact that we wish precisely that the reader engage in commerce with the senses. But we do require earnest meditation of a particular kind. And we do want prejudices left aside. By prejudices we mean particularly views of what philosophy is about, the meaning of different systems of philosophy which the reader might fancy to use as a term of comparison with what he expects to find here. We will not in fact be talking here about systems of philosophy: we will be talking about the reader, you, and asking you to attend to yourself, to ask yourself certain simple questions, to reach elementary answers.

First of all we hope that the reader is conscious: not a vain hope, since if you were unconscious you would certainly not be reading this book. Being conscious of course doesn't involve any type of looking at yourself. If you are looking at pictures in a gallery you are conscious: but that doesn't mean that there is an extra looking-at-yourself. Looking at pictures just happens

[1]R. Descartes, *A Discourse on Method*, Veitch's translation, Everyman, 1953, 73

3

to be that sort of activity which we call conscious. Again, you
are intelligently conscious when you are puzzling over a problem: you are intelligently conscious too, we hope, as you read
this book, and since our approach is unfamiliar you are perhaps
not a little puzzled. Are you?

The last question should halt you in your tracks. If you are
willing to meditate with us in earnest then you will have to
settle down to some serious self-attention. Am I puzzled? The
question is to be asked by the reader about himself. Its answering requires attention to himself on the part of the reader. Now,
that self-attention is not a matter of looking at oneself, as the
reader will find if he continues with us. For that self-attention
we have already used the word 'introspection' but that is just an
unfortunate limitation of language. At any rate we ask you to
answer certain simple questions about yourself and these questions and answers will involve some degree of what we call
self-attention.

First of all, do you ever wonder? Are you perhaps even now
wondering about what we are at and where it is all leading?
If so, then you will be able to answer our first question affirm-
atively: Yes, I wonder about this and that, and I am wondering
where all this is leading at the moment. So far, so good.

What, then, do you wonder about? For it would seem that
you just don't wonder in a vacuum. You may wonder about a
sudden noise, or about the meaning of a sentence in this book.
You may wonder about many things but certainly you will
admit that you have wondered on occasion about what you have
seen or heard etc., or even about something imagined. You
might well at this moment imagine the rainbow—did you ever
wonder about the rainbow and appeal to a physicist friend or
a textbook in order to satisfy your wonder? Your wonder
would be satisfied insofar as you reached some understanding
of why the rainbow appeared as it did, one might say, of *what* a
rainbow is. As we shall see better in the next chapter, Why-

and What–questions are closely related. At any rate your basic question to your physicist friend would be some form of the question, What is a rainbow? It is of course to the physicist that you go, for you expect him to understand light, and it is understanding you seek. When you yourself reach understanding you too will be able to explain: but before you understand you literally haven't an idea. In the present case what you are hoping to understand is the appearance of the rainbow, and depending on the pedagogical skill of your friend, your hope will not be in vain.

It is interesting in this context of trying to understand, or learn, or teach, to reflect on a famous passage in St Thomas's *Summa Theologica:*

> Anyone can find in his own experience that, whenever he tries to understand anything, he forms phantasms for himself, to serve as examples in which he may—by inspection, as it were—reach that which he is striving to understand. And for the same reason, when we wish to make anyone understand anything, we offer him examples from which he can form phantasms for himself, in order to understand.[2]

One might well pause here to consider the importance and relevance at all levels of education of the pedagogical principles implicit here.

So far we have centred our attention on wonder in one mode, wonder expressed in a What–question. That wonder, when satisfied, leaves one capable of defining or explaining. Now wonder expresses itself also in another mode: as an Is–question. Have you had experience of this mode? 'I wonder if it is raining?', 'Is smoking injurious to health?', etc. Wonder expressed in this mode is satisfied by an intelligent 'Yes' or 'No', or even by a 'Probably' or an 'I don't know'.

Next, you might consider how these two modes of wonder-

[2]Prima Pars, q. 84, a. 7

ing are related. While this might most easily be illustrated from science you might try reflecting on such a simple illustration as being woken up during the night by a scraping sound. You may start by wondering what woke you up, but let us say that you have got to the stage of asking, What is that scraping? A mouse? Notice here that there is no problem in such a simple case of searching for definition: you have already some description of what a mouse is. But is it a mouse? Yes or No? The intelligent thing is to get up, put on the light and inspect the room. And so on. It is for the reader to multiply examples and thus to appreciate that he wonders, that that wonder is related to experience, that it operates in two modes.

We will be concerned in the following two chapters with each of these modes in turn. But before tackling them in more detail it is worth while to reflect on the universality of this structured wonder. This structured wonder about experience, which you are discovering in yourself, is in fact something which you share with all men, be they of the present or the past, of the east or the west.[3] A classic debate in contemporary theology contrasts the mentality of the Hebrews and the Greeks. But in the light of their common sharing of structured wonder, that contrast reveals itself as not being fundamental. No doubt, the Hebrews, unlike the Greeks, did not turn to a discussion of wonder or of questions. But they asked questions, and one has only to work through a random section of the Bible, picking out the question-marks of a modern text, to appreciate that the questions are identifiably of two modes. What differentiates the questions and the answers and the two cultures is a larger issue: but the point you are asked to note and reflect on is that common structure of questioning.

However, we must emphasize that the reader's primary concern is with himself and his own operations of inquiry.

[3]Cf. F. E. Crowe, 'Neither Jew nor Greek, but One Human Nature and Operation in All', *Philippine Studies* (13), 1965, 456–517

We have spoken of structured wonder and we conclude this short chapter with a diagram which indicates that structure. We will have to deal in turn with the elements and their inter-relations as indicated, and so gradually reveal the significance of the pattern.

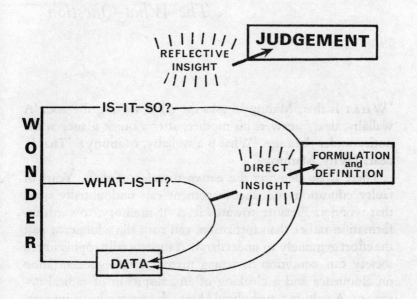

3

The What-Question

'WHAT is that, Mammy?' asks the child visiting the zoo. 'A wallaby, dear,' answers his mother, after a quick glance at the notice under the cage. 'What is a wallaby, Mammy?' 'That is, dear.' 'Why, Mammy?'

There is no denying the native wonder of man. Years of faulty education and discouragement can undoubtedly quell that wonder. Pressure towards feats of memory, towards information rather than formation, can rush the adolescent past the effort genuinely to understand. A superficially sophisticated society can condition its young members into concentration on eloquence and a cloaking of any suspicion of radical nescience. A culture which should know better can leave unquestioned the illusion that, while man does not understand everything, still he has a jolly good idea.

A discussion of decadence and bias is well beyond our limited scope. In the conclusion to chapter seven we will return briefly to these topics under the heading of personal authenticity and in chapter eight the social dimension will be touched on. Still, it is worth noting here that there are such problems and that they do not make any easier the task of appreciating the meaning of the What–question.

The visitor to the zoo can reach a certain contentment in being able to name the animals: knowing a name somehow gives confidence, power. But knowing the name and being able to describe the animal is a far cry from understanding it—as Socrates revealed in his own way to his contemporaries. It is our hope here to lead the reader some distance towards Socratic wisdom, towards the wisdom of authentic nescience. We would hope to bring you to appreciate the difference, the gap in question. It is important to appreciate that gap, to know that we are not God, that far from understanding everything about everything, we understand almost nothing about anything. Yet we do anticipate by our native wonder an understanding of everything, and that anticipation can be coupled with the illusions we have mentioned; understanding of the use of words can pass for the understanding of what the words denote.

It is through this gap that there proudly march the speculative gnostic and the practical magician. They anticipate scientific understanding of what things are and how results are to be produced. They anticipate the pure scientist's preoccupation with numbers and the applied scientist's preoccupation with tools. They are necessary factors in the dialetic development of human intelligence, for without their appearance and their eventual failure, men would not learn the necessity of effective criteria for determining when adequate insight actually has occurred. But because their efforts are prior to the discovery of those criteria, because their pure desire to know is not contrasted with all other desires, because names and heuristic anticipations can be mistaken for insights, because partial insights have the same generic character as full understanding, because the satisfaction of understanding can be mimicked by an air of profundity, a glow of self-importance, a power to command respectful attention, because the attainment of insight is a hidden event and its content a secret that does not admit communication, because other men worship understanding but are not secure enough in their own possession of it to challenge mistaken claims, the magician and then the gnostic have their day.[1]

As one moves up the hierarchy of the human sciences to theology one finds that the danger of such mythic thinking increases. Moreover, it is supported by common sense, whose voculabary it largely shares. The child can recite the Hail Mary not unintelligently: the man has every encouragement to fall into the illusion that he knows precisely what the Mother of God means.

Let us make an initial effort to appreciate the gap. Let us recall the rule for extracting square roots which no doubt you learned in school. A simple illustration will serve:

$$
\begin{array}{r}
\phantom{1\sqrt{1\ }} 1\ \ 3\ \ 2 \\
\hline
1\sqrt{1\ \ 74\ \ 24} \\
1 \\
23\quad 74 \\
69 \\
262\quad \ \ 524 \\
524 \\
\hline
\end{array}
$$

You recall the rule? The number whose square root is sought is divided into pairs of numbers starting from the unit end. These pairs are 'brought down' successively. Each time the number already reckoned, e.g. 13, is doubled and used to determine the next number in the square root, etc., etc. A little practice will refresh your memory and the process of getting square roots can become almost automatic. You can use the rule with ease. But our crucial question is, do you understand the rule, the *Why* of it? What does the procedure *mean*? You were taught how to use the rule at some stage, but it was not in fact ex-

[1]B. Lonergan, *Insight,* London and New York 1957, 542.

plained. Indeed the explanation may well have been beyond your teacher.

To ask you to remedy that defect at this stage and age may seem very much beside the point. You had hopes perhaps of a panoramic view of the world or the works of Lonergan, and now alas you find the path to wisdom strewn with square roots! A panoramic view indeed there is, but it can come only at the end of a long climb. Here we can only indicate how you might go about the first hard steps.

But note that we are not just interested in getting you to remedy a defect in your mathematical education. We would hope that you would now engage not just in mathematics but in metamathematics, the methodology of mathematics. Let us enlarge on this point.

We have provided you with a puzzle: what is the meaning of this rule for extracting square roots, why does it work? Now we wish you to solve this puzzle but during the procedure we wish you to have a dual interest. For we wish you not only to be interested in solving the problem, but also to be interested in how you go about doing so. We want you to add to the puzzle the question, 'How do I go about solving this puzzle?' You should have, in other words, a methodological interest in the procedure. You should be able to ask and answer such questions as: Am I conscious, wondering, using diagrams, adjusting diagrams ('disposing the phantasm', Aquinas might say), getting clues, hints, little insights?

You may well at this stage read on, thus showing that like so many others you have suffered the standard failure in education, the failure to learn how to read. Insofar as you understand everything we are talking about you have only to read to understand. Now you may well understand the rule for extracting square roots, but do you understand what we mean by introspective metamathematics? Please try it then before going on. If the rule for extracting square roots is too obvious, then you should be in a position to manufacture a rule for cube roots, and if you are to such an extent familiar with mathematics you should in fact have no trouble in finding data for metamathematics.

Now that you have at least tried, if not succeeded, let us look at how understanding of the rule may have emerged. Why pair off the numbers? Why double the results each time? Let us perhaps reverse the process, square the result. How—by straight multiplication? No—let us spread it out: the answer, 132, can be broken down into $100+30+2$, so instead of saying $[132]^2$ we can say $[100+30+2]^2$. You may not have remembered how to expand that, but with a little juggling you can arrive at the result:

$$[100+30+2]^2 = 100^2 + 30^2 + 2^2 + 2.100.30 + 2.100.2 + 2.30.2.$$

A clue that you might have got at this stage would relate the multiple '2' of the expansion to the doubling of the result at each stage. Notice here how the illustration was chosen help-fully to the extent that 132 does not include a repetition of a number: this helps for identification in the expansion. But notice also that it would have been more helpful to have had an illustration without the occurrence of the number '2': for, that '2' can be confused with the multiplying '2'. All this is related to Aquinas's and Aristotle's notion of modifying the diagram, disposing the phantasm, and to the role of the pedagogue in 'setting things up', so that the solution begins to 'stare the pupil in the face'.

Next, the expansion is recast by us to help you (in case you have failed):

$$[100+30+2]^2 = 100^2 + 2.100.30 + 30^2 + 2.100.2 + 2.30.2 + 2^2$$
$$= 100^2 + [2.100+30].30 + [2.100+2.30+2].2$$
$$= 100^2 + 230.30 + 262.2.$$

You may not have caught on even now: but don't give up, and don't hide behind the claim that really mathematics was never your line (this pronouncement is often made as if ignorance of mathematics was a special grace!). We appeal to you to try again. Insight is a very precious thing, and insight into little things can be extraordinarily significant.

If you have reached the understanding of this rule then you can shift from arithmetic to algebra, generalize it, etc., above all you can explain it pedagogically to someone else.

And perhaps now you have some insight into the difference between the use of the rule and the meaning of the rule. The instance has been given on the level of mathematics but it has its parallel in all other fields—it is for the reader to push that parallel. But especially it should be considered in the basic context of the use of words and the meaning of words.

One might reflect similarly on a variety of What–questions, what is acceleration?, what is heat?, what is malaria?, what is neurosis?, what is love?, what is man?, what is God? All along the line there is the possibility of identifying the nature and limitations of one's understanding. Let us double back our consideration on itself by noting that, just as the taxi-driver may claim to know quite well what acceleration is, just as the non-biologist may claim to know quite well what a dog is, so you may have tended to claim, till now, that you know quite well what understanding is. We are here concerned with bringing you to a rejection of that claim and to the beginnings of an understanding of your own understanding. The basic distinction is between experience or familiarity and understanding. Undoubtedly you have had experience of understanding before now: but till now you perhaps never raised the question, what is understanding?, in any serious sense.

We return to the more straightforward task of bringing you to appreciate the distinction between familiar experience and understanding. Again we take a simple piece of mathematics—it is for you to reach into your own experience for other possible sources of enlightenment. You might consider that we would be better employed discussing more relevant instances of the distinction; for instance, that familiarity with people's faces is a far cry from understanding people. But you might agree too easily with this, you might too easily obscure the radical difference between experiencing, seeing, etc., and understanding.

Consider then the familiar oval shape called an ellipse. What is an ellipse? You might answer: an oval shape, a plate looked at sideways, etc. But, like the child in the zoo, we might follow up with the question, Why? We are, in short, asking for the law of the ellipse, if you like, how is it made? Following up this last suggestion we give you a clue—and don't forget that your interest is methodological—an ellipse has two centres: Try two of your fingers in a loop of thread.

There will be those of course who read on here without pausing, those who find our little book fascinating but beside the point. A pity: for we certainly would not foist such illustrations on the public did we not think that the self-appropriation that they might bring was enormously relevant in our times. We recall J. L. Synge's comment on Jaques Hadamard's little book on the psychology of mathematicians: 'Such things may strike us strange and rather fascinating, a strand of queerness enlivening the dull desert of scientific thought, arid stretches of logic. We may dismiss them lightly and pass on to the serious consideration of what thought and understanding are in terms of the words that philosophers have been accustomed to use. But we may be quite wrong in this. We may miss the turning leading to an understanding of understanding.'[2]

Returning to our ellipse, we find that the successful drawing leads to a definition of an ellipse: the locus of points such that the sum of their distance from two fixed points remains constant. In symbols, $AP + BP = $ Constant, where A and B are fixed and P is a point on the locus. We have thus arrived at a

[2]J. L. Synge, *Science, Sense, and Nonsense*, London 1951, 112.

What–answer. Is it correct? In asking that question we anticipate the next section, on the Is–question, and the reader will
find it worthwhile to return to this passage when that section
has been reflected upon. Now, in fact, the definition is not
correct. Why? Recall that the coast of Ireland is the locus of
points equi-distant from a fixed point![3]

We could now possibly pause to spell out here what is so
densely expressed in Lonergan's *Insight*, 7–12. But we would
ask the reader to answer reflectively only the question, Can you
imagine the definition of an ellipse? Is seeing anything like understanding? We would hope that the reader would gradually
come to appreciate that there is no analogy whatever between
perceiving and answering a question be it a What–question or
an Is–question.

The reader will notice that the definition of an ellipse is rela-
tional, and that the relations are, so to speak, of parts of the
ellipse to each other.

Before reaching that definition we spoke of the ellipse in
terms of how it looked to us. This illustrates a general charac-
teristic of the shift to definition. Think of the question, What
is pressure? The immediate answer will be in terms of push and
pull. The answer in terms of the gas laws involves correlations
of correlations of correlations. The repetition is deliberate. Do
you recall the simple apparatus used? A volume of gas, a column
of mercury, a ruler, etc.? Now a ruler already involves a first
set of correlations—the reader should not take that for granted:
it is an opportunity for wonder and insight into measurement,
coupled with the possibility of self-attentive reflection. Then
there are the sequences of measurements of volumes and
pressures leading to a set of numbers such as:

P   30 40 50 60 70 80 90 · · · ·
V   1   9   7   6   5 $4\frac{1}{2}$ 4 · · · ·

[3]So the definition of an ellipse must include the fact that it is two-
dimensional. (Editor.)

One reaches the law from the clue gained by multiplying and intelligently neglecting random differences etc.

The reader is perhaps beginning to appreciate the flexibility and variability of insight, the manner in which intelligence can neglect just what is to be neglected and attend to what is relevant. No room here for some simple-minded view of abstraction in the modern world of differential calculus, surds, limitation theorems in mathematical logic, psychic illness and social illness. Intelligence can comfortably do mathematics with a green pen and have no difficulty in excluding green from the definition. But the procedure can be trickier, and so, a long scientific education may be needed to control the spontaneous anticipation of understanding. If the fractions between 0 and 1 can be put in one-one correspondence with the natural numbers, then surely the decimals between 0 and 1 can be put in similar correspondence? Indeed one might be inclined to say that the decimals might be easier to handle than the fractions. The problem here is to label the fractions—or decimals—so that for any given number the label can be produced,

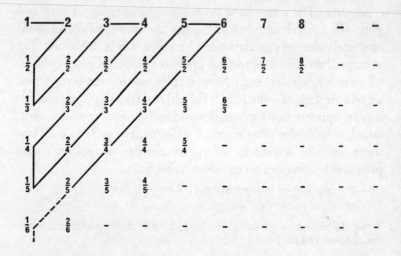

and vice versa. We might delay here to give hints, as in other examples, as to how to label the fractions. We go on immediately however to give a handy way of labelling all the positive rational numbers. The reader of course could profitably delay here and try for himself.

The trick is to lay out the rational numbers in a suitable array and then label them diagonal-wise as indicated (there is a minor problem of leaving out the repeats). Now, you may name a rational number—I can find its label; you name a label, I'll point out its number. (cf. diagram p. 30.)

Can we do the same for decimals? The simplest labelling would seem to be the following:

1. ·00000000000 . . . . .
2. ·10000000000 . . . . .
3. ·20000000000 . . . . .
4. ·30000000000 . . . . .

etc. etc.

Still, a little reflection reveals flaws in this list (does it?). Let's try another strategy: what we might call the mirror image method in that we keep subtracting ones from the decimal 'reversed'. The beginnings of the list will help the reader to grasp what we mean:

1.   ·99999999999 . . . . .
2.   ·89999999999 . . . . .
3.   ·79999999999 . . . . .
     . . . .
10. ·09999999999 . . . . .
11. ·98999999999 . . . . .

We may not in fact be too happy with that either. But we need not despair. There must surely be some way of lining up the decimals with the natural numbers. To admit that there isn't or couldn't be is to admit a certain lunacy into mathematics as if there were more numbers than could be counted.

Let us assume that we have a suitable list, something like the two suggested. Now make a new decimal by taking the first number from the first decimal, the second from the second, and so on. Change each of these by, say, one. [The acute reader will note a problem here.] Now we have a new decimal which differs from all those in our supposed complete list. Something of an inverse insight!

One last instance of twisted insight may be both of interest and of profit. Aristotle did not discover statistical science. But let us see how he might have. Suppose he noted in his evening paper that Peripetes was killed by a falling slate in Athens. A week later Alciabiades is similarly killed and the event is noted by Aristotle. So he continues and begins to count: not in itself a very significant procedure, not apparently leading anywhere. Suppose at any rate that he ends up with the facts that in a sequence of months,

6 7 5 6 8 5 7 5 6

people had been killed by falling slates. As Kepler had the data on Mars before him for many years, so Aristotle might have had such a list before him for years. But the trick is, intelligent neglect of the random. The neglect leads to an understanding of the ideal, the average—here 6—about which the numbers oscillate. How obvious when it is explained! Yet it was not for centuries that the relevant insights occured. That is the sort of thing that the slow, painfully slow development of man's understanding involves. Nowadays statistical methods are a commonplace in science. It is quite another thing to understand introspectively what statistical method is, how it differs from and complements classical method, etc. Such an understanding hardly belongs to the first steps of methodology, so we come here to a suitably abrupt halt.

If the reader will pause and reflect on our discussion so far he may perhaps arrive at the suspicion that we have been cheating a little. In a certain sense he would be correct. In our early instances of What–questions we stressed correlations, properties if you like. But properties are always properties *of*. There is an insight involved here, which is, one might say, so spontaneous that it is regularly neglected if not worse. It is for instance neglected in the current debate about transubstantiation. It is the insight associated with the notion of thing, substance. We hesitate to venture into this delicate region with its demand for serious and prolonged self-attention. Perhaps however we may permit ourselves a helpful fable. It is about a man called Jonah. Jonah wakes up lying on his back feeling sick. The place is pitch dark, smelly, damp. He feels with his hands the damp, mossy, surface around him. He gets to his feet and the whole place sways about. He shines his pocket torch around: he is in some sort of cave, reddish-coloured, with odd projections and pieces of bone around. Then it dawns on him ... I'm in a whale! Now, note that the 'dawning' added nothing to the data beyond the unity-identity-wholeness of one thing (we speak loosely—obviously it pulls in his understanding of whales). Was his insight verified and how was it verified? Note that we think of many 'things' as things . . . The Germans probably think of their spectacles as a thing, 'meine Brille'; do you? You can think of a car as a thing: is it? How do you know?

We might go on here to discuss the role of scientists in determining what are things, etc., etc., but we think it best to bring this rambling chapter to a close with our fable. In that way we can add emphasis to our claim that we are strictly giving a survey of the foothills of introspective methodology, that there is no short or easy way up the slope.

4

The Is-Question

GUILTY or not Guilty: that question does not ask for a definition, but for a verdict, a Yes or a No. No doubt when the jury retire to consider the case many of them may not be at all clear on the evidence. As they debate the issue among themselves they come to understand better the events and circumstances, the motives and the opportunities. But there comes that stage when questions about the nature of the case yield to that attitude of mind which seeks to bring forth judgement: Guilty? Yes or No?

The jury retire to the jury room precisely to bring forth a judgement of this type. Judgement rests with them and they appreciate a responsibility and the element of personal commitment involved. They are selected as intelligent and unbiased, and their judgement is eventually accepted as fitting the facts, as strictly objective. They do not decide in the strict sense of that word that the person is guilty or not: the judgement of guilt directly relates to what actually happened, not to what they would like to have happened. Moreover the happening includes not just external activities and circumstances, but such intangible elements as motives and sanity. Judgement then is not just a matter of looking in some mysterious way at the facts, what happened. It is, as it were, removed from the visible, the audible, the appearances. It lies within intelligence, within an understanding of the case in all its aspects, and when each jury member commits himself on the case he does so with the detachment of intelligence, with a nod of the head rather than a pointing of the finger. This last opposition, if you like, brings out the difference between answering a question and perceiving: there is no parallel between these. Again, the juror expects his judgement to be respected. To challenge a man's judgement is to come near to the bone. As de la Rochefoucauld says, 'Everybody complains of his memory, but nobody of his judgement'.[1] One often hears the remark, 'I have a very poor memory,' but rarely are we tempted to say, 'I have very poor judgement.'

It is worth while reflecting on the odd statement that a judgement is invisible. It may be about appearances, but it is not an appearance. It has the remoteness of understanding from appearances. As earlier we pointed out that one cannot imagine the definition of a circle or an ellipse, so here we note that judgement is no more imaginable. Judgement, and the truth reached in judgement, is in people's minds and in people's minds only. I may express my judgement in a written sentence, but the written sentence is not true or false. The writing of itself is just a series of marks on paper—both the meaning and the truth are in my mind. One might find it helpful to consider the old paradox of the written sentence, 'This sentence is false.' Is it? If it is, then it is true, and vice versa. Again one might consider the question of judgement in relation to the truths in the Bible. In what sense are there truths in the Bible? Certainly not in the sense that between any two of the dots that we call full stops there lies a truth. Truth, the fruit of judgement, is found only in a mind.

The procedure in the jury room in coming to judgement has the same generic structure as the procedure in a science of verifying some theory, some hypothesis. In both cases one moves

[1] *Maxims,* translated by L. W. Rancock, Penguin, 1967, Maxim 89.

from data to some understanding of the data which must be adequately checked. To understand the nature of that checking is to understand the nature of judgement or verification.

It is clear enough both from our illustration of the jury and from our previous considerations of the What–question about experience, that judgement somehow depends on these other levels and completes them. One cannot ask an intelligent Is–question without having a What–answer. 'Is the kettle boiling?' requires, if it is to be answered, that the person questioned understands by his common sense what a kettle is, what boiling means. Indeed it requires a lot more: the question may have arisen from hearing a whistling in the kitchen, and the answering comes through a use of many habits of understanding and behaviour which we scarcely notice. In the general case one can say that judgement requires a background of other knowledge and understanding. Is this not the reason why we call in the expert? We go to the doctor that he may judge our health and our sickness and of course that we may be cured. We may be very sick but feeling sick and understanding the sickness are two radically different things. So we may go to the doctor and ask, for example, 'Is it arthritis, doctor?' We have some vague notion of the connection between arthritis and stiffness, but it is the doctor who is in a position to judge, for he understands to some extent the meaning of arthritis. To judge, of course, he must look, listen, etc., but the doctor's looking is very different from the patient's looking. It is backed by understanding. Again, the physicist trying to verify some elaborate theory may end up looking at a dial—but it is the meaning, the significance, of the place of the needle on the dial, that is important. One might consider similarly judgements about the economy, about people, etc.

As yet, however, we haven't tackled directly the question, What is a judgement? We may say immediately of course that it can be tackled adequately only by the same method as used in tackling the What–question. Judgement is something that occurs in us regularly. To answer the question, 'What is judgement?' requires that we turn our attention to that type of occurrence in us. So far here we have been indicating the role of intelligence in judgement in a general and familiar way. But it is quite another matter, indeed a matter of years of effort, to proceed self-attentively to an understanding of the reflective insight which gives rise to the answer to the Is–question.

Let us return to the jury room. The evidence has been heard. The evidence has been understood. At this stage the central interest of the jury is the question, 'Is the evidence sufficient?' The basic problem is to grasp the sufficiency of the evidence— or its insufficiency. So the jury engages in weighing the evidence But what do we mean by weighing the evidence? This is the problem facing us if we are to understand the reflective insight which gives rise to judgement.

Now there is little hope of our readers reaching an adequate appreciation of that understanding unless they are willing to attend to themselves in their own significant judgements. By significant judgements we mean judgements which are not just imaginary, vague considerations of general sentences etc. To be significant does not require that a judgement be elaborate or complicated. Thus if you are asked 'Is the door behind you open?' then you react in a certain way to reach the answer, Yes or No. You look around. You see. But, if you attend to yourself you will notice that the looking round was done intelligently—a dog, if asked the same question, might just wag his tail. Again, the seeing was intelligent. No doubt mere seeing was part of the judging, but the centre of the stage was occupied by intelligence. What leads to the judgement, 'It is closed,' is not mere seeing, but the grasp of the sufficiency of the seeing. Undoubtedly that may seem odd to more than a few. After all, you may only have to look! Our next chapter will, we hope, help to undermine that view.

It is, at any rate, judgements of this type that we would wish the reader to reflect upon initially—judgements, that is, concerning simple matters of fact. 'Is the wind from the north?', 'Is there a chance of recovery?': questions like these give rise to such judgements of fact. We may profitably write these questions in another form, thus bringing out clearly a certain aspect of judgement: 'The wind is from the north?' 'There is a chance of recovery?'. One may note immediately that the transition to judgement consists, in some way, in merely removing the question mark. The defining meaning is already there: Yes or No adds nothing to it. The transition, we say, is effected by the grasp of the sufficiency of the evidence, an intelligent grasp which satisfies the wonder expressed in the question. But what is this grasp, and what does it grasp?

Consider again the question, 'The wind is from the north?'. To eliminate the question-mark one might well go out, face in a known direction and put a wet finger in the air. Why? Because these activities are intelligently appreciated as being relevant to the removal of the question-mark. They are grasped one might say as conditions which if fulfilled will lead to the intelligent removal of the question mark, to the assertion 'The wind is from the north.' First we grasp the prospective judgement, but we grasp also conditions for its assertion and their link with the prospective judgement, and we seek to grasp their actual fulfilment.

Now it is important to note that the conditions are not like premises from which one deduces the required judgement. The conditions invariably involve a return to data which is neither judgement nor understanding. The cold feeling on one side of a wet finger is not a judgement but a feeling, about which no doubt we judge easily. Thus our prospective judgement does in fact involve such easy judgements as this. But as one pushes the issue back, say, to the question 'Is the far side of my finger cold?', one comes closer to appreciating the manner in which the conditions involve mere data.

Moving, then, from the Is–question to the judgement involves grasping the link between the prospective judgement and its conditions, some of which will be sensible, visible, audible, etc., and further, the grasping of the fulfilment of these conditions. We may formulate that procedure as follows:

If my raised wet finger feels colder on the north side; then the wind is from the north,
But my raised wet finger feels colder on the north side,
Therefore the wind is from the north.

The major premise here expresses an understanding of the link between the prospective judgement and a sufficient condition; the minor premise expresses the grasp of the fulfilment of that condition. The minor premise here of course expresses another judgement: on this we have already commented. But in the more basic case the fulfilment of the conditions is appreciated in a prejudgemental fashion leading, as we said, to the elimination of the question-mark from the prospective judgement. If there were not such prejudgemental grasp of the fulfilled conditions on the level of the given, of data, then we would land back in the problem of infinite regress. Thus, the minor premise above would require another minor premise, X, in a new syllogism:

If X, then my raised wet finger feels colder on the north side, and X,
Therefore my raised wet finger feels colder on the north side.

And so *ad infinitum*.

However, concluding to the existence of prejudgemental insight into fulfilling conditions etc. does not rest on an argument such as this: it rests on the experience of such insight in ourselves. It is for the reader to engage in that experience with various judgements and to endeavour to understand its nature. It is only by going over and over the process self-attentively that such understanding can be reached. The illustrations we have taken have been simple judgements of fact, but the reader may venture into more difficult judgements such as judgements of science or mathematics, to find the same basic structure and further complexities.

A simple comment which may save the reader a variety of apparent difficulties concerns the little word 'is'. The occurrence of this little word in a sentence does not always connote a judgement: it occurs also regularly in definitions such as, 'A dog is an animal.' Such definitions belong, in our terms, to the second level of cognitional structure. The 'is' in such definitions is, so to speak, synthetic, holding-together. It can be clearly distinguished from the 'is' which occurs in judgements such as, 'This dog is dead.' In judgement the 'is' is associated with positing or rejecting, with saying what in fact is the real state of affairs.

Again the reader may raise the question of the certainty of particular judgements. It is a question of interest and importance, but could at this elementary stage be a source of confusion and distraction. Let us remark then that human certainty is not a black and white affair—nor indeed an affair of three degrees, moral certainty, physical certainty and metaphysical certainty. Certainty in fact is a spectrum affair: how certain am I? Certain enough in a given case, less certain in another. In this connection one may mention that there is difficulty concerning the use of the word 'probability' in relation to judgement. When we say that our judgement is probably correct we express the fact that the content of the judgement is not quite as unconditioned as would be the case in a certain judgement. The fulfilment of the conditions may be problematic: 'He is probably still in his office—at least he was when I phoned a few minutes ago.' Probability in this sense, like certainty, refers to the content. There is on the other hand the probability which we touched on earlier by way of illustration of insight. That probability is a ratio, frequency, and it is clearly distinguishable from the probability of a judgement. Like the difficulty with 'is', this difficulty can be summarily despatched by noting the relation of the two senses of probability to the two levels of cognitional structure: frequency-probability belongs primarily to the second level as content of a theory; probability of judgement belongs to the third level as quality of its content.

Finally, if the reader investigates further the jury coming to judgement, he will appreciate that their judgement is not merely a matter of their own experience and understanding. They have listened to witnesses, reliable and less reliable. They have accepted evidence and other people's judgements on certain matters. In a word, their judgement is meshed with a complex of beliefs. Now judgement is one way of possessing the truth, belief is another and complementary way. In this section we have been raising in an elementary way the question, What is judgement? It is another and more difficult matter to face the problem, What is belief? We will return to it in chapter eight.

In an appendix to the book we have added a consideration of various puzzles which should help the reader towards an appreciation in general of the method of self-attention, and in particular of disposing the 'clues', understanding, checking, etc. Obviously any instance of understanding is a datum for introspective methodology. It is for the reader to discover what instances best whet his appetite for that science.

5

Inside-Out

What is the environment? The answer to this question comes promptly enough—the environment is 'out-there'. It is this book, the walls of this room, the people passing to and fro; it is everything that is outside of us. This answer is of course a rational one, but it is founded upon an elaborate system of inferences developed through a lifetime of experiencing. If a forefinger is placed along the lower ridge of the eyesocket so that its tip is against the nose and the other eye is covered, pressing the eyeball gently and moving it up and down will cause the environment to jump back and forth. Now this is manifestly unreasonable! Any force sufficient to shake the room would also have been felt as vibration. But what, then, is the explanation of this phenomenon?[1]

The author goes on to give his explanation of this phenomenon which summarily is given in the remark that behaviourally, the environment is a pattern of neural energies in the central nervous system. We are not here embarking on an excursus into experimental psychology, though indeed we might well draw on its findings to strengthen our pedagogical strategy. But we are centrally interested in that basic question, 'What is

[1]Charles E. Osgood, *Method and Theory in Experimental Psychology*, New York 1953, 1.

the environment?', and this first illustration that Osgood gives of rocking the room may help the reader to rock that spontaneous conviction that reality is 'out there'. For we suspect that, even though you have followed our arguments and illustrations so far, you may well have missed a central point, what we like to call the Bridge of Asses in methodology. You may well insist on agreeing with us that correct, verified understanding is knowledge of what is real and still be firm in the conviction that what is real is what is 'out there'. And so, here we will try to correct that view, by illustration and illusion, by parable and paradox.

Let us put the matter this way. Till now we have been describing and sketchily explaining a particular type of human activity called knowing. We have tried to get you to establish that there are three basic components, that the process of knowing is a three storied process. Now this activity is going on in you, the organism. A diagram will help, but please remember that it is only a diagram, a crutch, to help you to understand yourself. Again many of our remarks are of the same type— twisted truths, efforts to bring you through difficult insights: to take them out of that context and to use them for philosophic mud-slinging would be to miss the point. The diagram on page 44 represents you, the organism. We have put a three floored box inside to indicate the activity of knowing which we have discussed in the last three chapters. We might compare that activity to a process of digestion. What is being digested? Might we suggest, the environment? In fact we are representing the sensitive integration by the lower box: W and the arrow indicate the 'enzyme' wonder and its driving towards judgement through the What– and Is–questions. To complete our description of the diagram there are the two bumps on the organism to represent the eyeballs. Certainly there are many and varied receptors on and in the organism, but we find it convenient to concentrate our attack on the odd view of realism with which we associate the name 'myth of the eyeballs'.

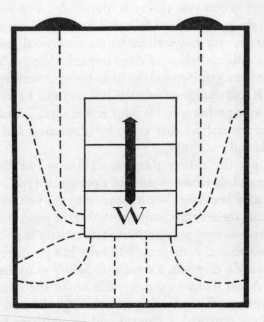

Now if the reader will indulge in the experiment suggested in the quotation from Osgood he or she will find that the environment rocks. We ask you to attend to that experience and to overcome the tendency to claim that obviously the real room isn't rocking but the appearances are disturbed. That of course is one of our twisted suggestions! What we are trying to counteract is the tendency to deny that the rocking is 'out there'. The rocking is, we hope you agree, very definitely 'out there'.

A parallel experiment consists in taking off your spectacles (if you wear spectacles) or putting on someone else's (if you don't). In this case the environment gets hazy. Again we ask you to attend. You are looking at, say, legible print on distant book titles. You remove or put on spectacles—and the print gets hazy: what is hazy is what is 'out there'. One might say that the organism is such that the bottom box in our diagram, the sensitive integration, has an extrojected quality, providing an environment for the animal. Let us try some logic on it. Obviously the spectacles do not affect anything beyond the lenses: it is only when the light hits the lens on its path to the eyes that it is turned off its tracks. Then the logic is simple:

What the spectacles affect is not beyond the lenses;
What the spectacles affect is the 'out there' environment;
Therefore the 'out there' environment is not beyond the lenses.

Are we beginning to shake your sense of reality? You may continue to shake it by reflecting on various other experiences and illusions, your own and others. The mental patient who sees huge spiders coming down the wall, 'out there', the patient with the amputated leg and the itching toes, mirages, sticks 'out there bent' in water, etc., etc.

But you may not like our efforts to shake your sense of reality. You may feel that we are leading you into a strange subjectivism: that we are confining you within your own skin. Indeed we *are* confining you within your own skin: to quote Tennessee Williams, 'We are all condemned to solitary confinement within our own skins.' At any rate insofar as you do not like our efforts you will argue against them, you will explain away our illustrations. Now in getting you thus to argue we consider that we have in fact boxed you in thoroughly. Let us explain this by making clear first our own position.

Our own position rests on a fundamental assumption: that what is real is reached by correctly understanding experience. Correctly understanding experience is a process that goes on in the human organism. Its final fruit we may call the known. We assume an identity between the known and the real. Now obviously that identity is not ontological: knowing a cow is not having a cow in the mind. The identity is technically called intentional. But this is not the important point for you: the important point is to appreciate that there is no way whatsoever of comparing your activity of knowing with a reality known. As if, you might say, there was some possibility of a super-look, of getting outside your own skin!

The nice thing about our assumption is that it is inescapable. Certainly, you can't argue your way out of it without assuming it. For what is argument but the assumption that it is correct understanding that wins the day! Many philosophers have produced various and curious views of what is real and what is not; but they would all insist that their views were intelligent and reasonable and squared with what was given. With this in mind, you may return now to the task of arguing your way out of the view given above. Negatively expressed, that view denies that the environment 'out there' is the real; positively expressed, it claims that the real is what is reached by correctly understanding experience. Experience is a component, only a component, of knowing.

Now you may well be with us all the way and still be inclined to claim that the known is in some way *like* the experienced, the environment 'out there'. No: the known is not similar to the 'out there'. You moved towards admitting this indeed when you conceded in chapter three that you couldn't imagine the definition of the ellipse. The real is no more imaginable. The known elephant is not *like* the seen elephant: and the real elephant is the known elephant (or to-be-known elephant, of course!).

We will continue this discussion from another angle in the next chapter. We may conclude this one with a quotation which neatly recalls the first quotation of this chapter and answers the question posed there, but within a wider context:

A useful preliminary is to note that animals know, not

merely phenomena, but things: dogs know their masters, bones, other dogs, and not merely the appearance of these things. Now this sensitive integration of sensible data also exists in the human animal and even in the human philosopher. Take it as knowledge of reality, and there results the secular contrast between the solid sense of reality and the bloodless categories of the mind. Accept the sense of reality as criterion of reality, and you are a materialist, sensist, positivist, pragmatist, sentimentalist, and so on, as you please. Accept reason as a criterion but retain the sense of reality as what gives meaning to the term 'real', and you are an idealist; for, like the sense of reality, the reality defined by it is non-rational. In so far as I grasp it, the Thomist position is the clear-headed third position: reason is the criterion and, as well, it is reason—not the sense of reality—that gives meaning to the term 'real'. The real is what is; and 'what is' is known in the rational act, judgement.[2]

[2]B. Lonergan, *Verbum: Word and Idea in Aquinas,* Notre Dame 1967, 7.

6

Strange Structured Realism

THE foregoing chapter ended with a quotation that could well become a slogan: ' "What is" is known in the rational act, judgement'. It is easy to repeat. It is less easy to understand, to appropriate. Yet to grasp this point is crucial. If it is the Bridge of Asses, it is also the Rubicon. It is here that philosophies and philosophers most conspicuously divide. It is here that one crosses to the basic position of critical structured realism. Our central concern is neither philosophies nor philosophers but ourselves in our intellectual conversion and so once more we turn to the investigation of the data of our consciousness, with further hints from another angle. We may take the long quotation that concluded the foregoing chapter as our guide.

'A useful preliminary is to note that animals know, not merely phenomena, but things: dogs know their masters, bones, other dogs, and not merely the appearances of these things'. Why is this a useful preliminary? Why is it anything more than a passing observation? Crucial is the assertion, 'animals know things'. But what does 'know' mean here? It is worth noting that 'strictly, one will distinguish animal, human, angelic and divine knowing, and one will investigate what in each case is necessary and sufficient for an instance of knowing.'[1]

[1] B. Lonergan, 'Cognitional Structure', *Collection*, London and New York 1967, 224.

What is sufficient for an instance of animal knowing is not sufficient for an instance of human knowing. Dogs, then, know things, not merely phenomena, but animal knowing is not human knowing. Still, the sensitive integration of sensible data, which is central to the animal knowing, studied by animal psychologists, occurs also in men, but in men it is not knowing, it is a component in knowing.

Perhaps we are now in a position to tackle the niggling question which often arises in this context: when I see a man do I not know a man? And if I do not know him, is what I see an illusion? The answer to this twofold question involves a grasp of its ambiguity. When I see a man I do not necessarily know him, not because what I see is illusory, but because merely seeing is not human knowing. When I see a man is it the real man I see? Yes, you see the real man, not an illusion, but if you are merely seeing you do not yet know the real man. Further, if you are merely seeing, you do not know that it is the real man that you are seeing, for to know that it is the real man that you are seeing is not merely to see but to know, and to know to some extent what seeing is.

Once you leave behind the crude naïve realist or the empiricist position which accepts the sense of reality as the criterion of reality, which considers that in order to know you have merely to look, another position may attract you, ensnare you. The real elephant is not what is reached in seeing; the real is beyond seeing and sense; the real is unreachable. Still, the real is surely reachable. You accept that there is something beyond seeing, but now you are tempted to think of the beyond in the same way as you think of seeing. You may presume that you must look beyond with the mind. But let us keep more here to the problem of seeing. Since the higher kind of seeing, the going beyond sense, leaves sense behind, you may then be tempted to claim that what you see is appearance, and what is real is beyond it. So the incoherence mounts. But let us halt the illustration here. The fact is that sense does not know appearance, any more than sense knows reality. 'By our senses we are given, not appearance, not reality, but data.'[2]

If I claim in a particular case that when I look I see the real man, that is a judgement about the kind of activity that this seeing is. If I claim that when I look I see the appearance only, then that equally is a judgement about the nature of the seeing. The two exclude each other, but the issue between them is not to be decided merely by looking, but by inquiring into the nature of the seeing which is occurring. A central problem for the reader is to keep his attention on such occurring, on seeing and on inquiry in himself: it is all too easy to slide into a detached discussion where 'appearance' and 'reality' have no clear meaning, and the sources of meaning are neglected.

Again, we may recall that the known elephant is not like the seen elephant, not because the known elephant is more like something else, but because knowing is not like seeing. The known watch is not like the seen watch, not because the watch that I see is not the real watch, but once again because knowing is not like seeing, not at all like seeing, or hearing, or perceiving: between the answer to an Is–question and a percept there is no analogy.

Since this is an extremely difficult problem, we are trying by moving around the area to evoke in each reader some flash of understanding that would initiate him into appreciating how strange, while true, our position on reality is. We ourselves have only gradually, and each of us in his individual way, come to grips with it. But each reader should be on the look-out for personal clues to the relevant flashes of understanding in himself. To one of us such a flash of understanding occurred one day while walking: a cat crossed the path and the realization came that the real cat was seen, known to be seen, but not known, that to know the real cat would take an enormous effort, an

[2]*Op. cit.*, 235.

effort which is organized in that cooperative intellectual inquiry which is known as animal psychology. St Thomas Aquinas was well aware of such a point when he wrote in his commentary on St John's Gospel that to know what a stone was required not merely seeing but inquiry.[3] To the other author the oddities of critical realism only began to manifest themselves after four years of mathematical science and two years of philosophy: beginning from the gradual realization of what is ultimately crystallized in chapter five, moving slowly to an appreciation of what reflective understanding is. F. E. Crowe remarked once to the latter that it took him years to appreciate the nature of judgement. These concrete indications of aspects of slow intellectual conversion should both encourage the reader to patience and perseverance in the effort to understand understanding and make him very cautious of concluding that this critical realism is patent. 'It may be possible to miss the point here, despite the recurrent references to the polymorphism of human consciousness and the repeated castigation of the view that intellectual knowing is merely taking an intellectual look. But it seems rather important not to miss it; I should say there is an intellectual purification that stands to intellectual development somewhat as ascetical purification stands to advance in charity, and that intellectual purification requires a well-defined distinction between intellectual knowing and looking, between verification and imagination, between the objectivity that is based on intelligent inquiry and critical reflection and the objectivity for which animal extroversion serves as model.'[4]

How then do we know the real? In the present chapter we have centred attention on the question of sense, on the negative judgement that reality is not known by sense alone. But

[3]*In Joan.*, cap. I, lect. I.
[4]F. E. Crowe S.J., 'The Origin and Scope of Bernard Lonergan's *Insight*', *Sciences Ecclesiastiques* (IX) 1957, 265.

neither is reality known by understanding alone, for we always understand some data, and our understanding has to be checked. Not by judgement alone, because we always judge about whether or not our view or theory fits the data. But it is judgement that concludes the dynamic movement, that closes the structure, it is in judgement that we at last come to know, to know the real, what in fact is the case, it is in judgement that we reach intentional isomorphic structured identity with the real.

In these last few chapters especially we have tried to build a bridge across the Rubicon. This is the issue that divides the empiricists, for whom the real is known by sense, from the idealists, for whom the appearance, but not the real, is reached by sense, and these two from the critical realist for whom the real is reached in true judgement. But, for us more important, it is an issue which in some sense divides the reader from himself.

We have been trying to come to grips with the question, How do we know?, and in that context we have, in a curious fashion, defined reality. We have, if you like, put forward the assumption that reality is what is to be reached in true judgement. This does not settle what reality is in detail, but it does relate knowing to reality, and if the real is known in true judgement, then the whole of reality will be known in the complete set of true judgements. Once again, from another angle, we have reached the conclusion which is not the conclusion of an argument but an inescapable hypothesis. Its inescapability is encountered in performance. It may seem to be only a theory, yet to raise any question of its correctness is to presuppose its validity as the correct theory. There is no question here of comparison with other views. The comparison is with performance.

Again, the notion of a more elemental comparison pervades some empiricist and naïve realist views. There is the tendency to appeal to some type of elementary observation to check one's judgement with a reality reached in some other manner. On our position there is no possibility of comparing judgement with reality, since before reaching judgement we have not reached reality. Nor is there a question of merely observing, since direct understanding, which we are judging about, goes beyond data to intelligibility. Recall the form of the question for judgement. We may put it in the form, Does the theory fit the data? In this way one may note that there is, if you like comparison, but the comparison is not between judgement and reality, but between data and theory. In verifying we ask if the theory fits the data, if it covers all the data, if it covers only the data, etc. etc.—where the ecteteras connote one's movement towards grasp of sufficiency. As we remarked earlier, the movement of judgement is to discovery of what evidence would be sufficient and whether such sufficient evidence occurs. The focus of judgement is the grasp of such sufficiency, one's personal appreciation of sufficiency. It is here, indeed, that the personal character of human knowing appears most clearly. Only you can answer these questions for yourself, only you can terminate the movement to judgement.

You are perhaps beginning to appreciate this rational act, this Yes which affirms existence. You may even have begun to appreciate the elementary fact that judgement as a component in knowing reaches existence not by understanding it but by grasping the sufficiency of the evidence for it. In that sense we do not understand What existence is—but that is a deeper question which would carry us beyond the scope of this little book.

In this chapter we have added to our hints on the nature of knowing. We have talked of the problem of conversion and of the strangeness of critical realism. It is a strangeness the discovery of which one remembers, a strangeness too which remains. It is a realism that is not some vague but secure middle position between materialism and idealism.

Unless one breaks the duality in one's knowing, one doubts
that understanding correctly is knowing. Under the pressure
of that doubt, either one will sink into the bog of a knowing
that is without understanding, or else one will cling to understanding but sacrifice knowing on the altar of an immanen-
tism, an idealism, a relativism. From the horns of that dil-
emma one escapes only through the discovery (and one
has not made it yet if one has no clear memory of its startling
strangeness) that there are two quite different realisms, that
there is an incoherent realism, half animal and half human,
that poses as a half-way house between materialism and
idealism and, on the other hand, that there is an intelligent
and reasonable realism between which and materialism the
half-way house is idealism.[5]

[5]B. Lonergan, *Insight,* xxviii.

7

Metaethics

NEEDLESS to say we cannot hope to bring the reader in this short chapter to a sufficient appreciation of the methodology of ethics. The considerations of metaethics ultimately involve, indeed, both a theological dimension and the whole range of the human sciences. But we will be satisfied if we bring you here to grasp in your own decisions and doings a recurrence of the three levels already discussed, but now in a new context or with the addition of a new dimension. That new dimension is indicated in the diagram below by the addition of a single line

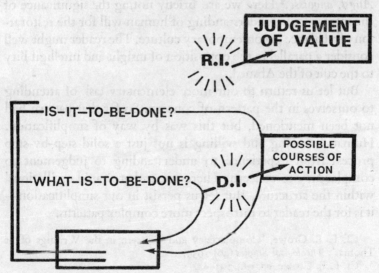

to the diagram at the end of chapter two. That single line denotes human will and willingness—your will of course—and the change in question-type denotes that we are dealing with what we call the pattern of concern.

This pattern of concern occurs when we are up and doing, or about to be so. It is not to be confused with anxiety, any more than its opposite, complacency, is to be confused with laziness. Both 'complacency' and 'concern' are in fact technical words.[1] The meaning of 'complacency' is perhaps best got at by reflecting on quiet enjoyment: for example, when one is enjoying a good film, a good book. It is an 'all's well' attitude. It is easier to reach some notion of 'concern', for it occurs when we are up and doing. It represents a 'What's-to-be-done?' attitude. Now a 'What's-to-be-done?' attitude, to be wholesome, must be based on a fundamental complacency, a *consent to being*, to the given state of affairs as a starting point. When it is not wholesome—as it is not, for example, in certain existentialist patterns of thought—then concern topples over into anxiety, *Angst, angoisse*.[2] Here we are briefly noting the significance of the introspective understanding of human will for the restoration of a balance in contemporary culture. The reader might well consider a parallel in the opposition of insight and intelligibility to the cult of the Absurd.

But let us return to our more elementary task of attending to ourselves in the pattern of concern. So far that pattern had not been mentioned, but this was by way of simplification. Human knowing and willing is not just a solid step-by-step process from experience to understanding to judgement to complacency to concern. There are, rather, 'rapid oscillations' within the structure. But let us persist in our simplification— it is for the reader to introspect more complex patterns.

[1]Cf. F. E. Crowe, 'Complacency and Concern in the Writings of St Thomas', *Theological Studies* (20) 1959.
[2]Cf. F. E. Crowe, *op. cit.*, 363–82.

Let us consider then a simple switch from a pattern of complacency to one of concern. You are driving along a pleasant country road, with appropriate breeze and sunshine, and a tyre blows. There is a distinct change of pattern, of attitude. Wonder enters a new phase: but it is still your same wonder with its same two basic expressions in What– and Is–questions. When you have taken in the basic situation your dominant question is 'What's to be done?'. The answer to that question will regularly be a set of possible modes of operation: so, one could walk back to the garage passed earlier, or one could set to work oneself, and so on. Like all What–answers, these are the result of insight, and very clearly insight into the given situation. But what possible course of action is to follow? That is another question, which in respect to any possible course of action may be phrased, 'Is it to be done?'

Continually here we remind you to self-attend in examples of such questions. It is all too easy to read on, to miss the point. The point is that we are trying to draw your attention to your own experience of decision, that you may wonder about its nature, begin to understand it. Now the question, 'Is it to be done?' is very near the focus of decision. 'Is such and such a possible course of action to be realized by me here and now?': that is a question demanding reflective insight. Insofar as the required insight occurs and results in a Yes, then, insofar as one is reasonable, the decision follows, one is on the move. The decision, of course, does not always follow, but that failure is not something to be explained. Failure in decision is failure to be reasonable, and attempts to explain that unreasonableness are attempts to put reason where there is none. Such attempts normally are called rationalizations.

If the reader suspects that we are in an unusually difficult region here, he is correct. Introspective understanding of the will is a delicate operation and the region of methodology dealing with it is barely in its infancy. But as we noted in chapter one regarding Aquinas's programme for understanding understanding so here we note that the parallel programme for understanding the will was not unknown to him. In an article of the *Summa Theologica* entitled 'Whether the intellect understands the act of will' he concludes by programming that investigation: 'And so the philosopher can say, "the will is in the reason". Now, if something is present intelligibly in an intelligent being it follows that it is understood by that intelligent being. Therefore the act of the will is understood by the intellect inasmuch as [a] one perceives *that* one wills, [b] one knows the nature of that act and subsequently [c] the nature of its principle which is the habit or potency.'[3] The reader interested in pushing forward with that programme would find helpful data in the works of F. E. Crowe.[4] Here, as usual, we can only give random hints.

The most important point to reflect on perhaps is the difference between the simple Is–question and the Is-it-to-be-done question. That difference may be expressed as a difference of context: one's interest has been expanded from what is actually the case to what might be the case. One appreciates that expansion best, obviously, when the realization of the might-be involves one's own activity. We will not spell out the expansion here,[5] but in chapter nine we give a single detailed illustration of the movement to decision.

Even our skimpy treatment should enable you to appreciate vaguely the recurrence of the basic three levels within this new context. That new context is the context of human doing, of will and willingness. It is from that experienced context that the word 'good' gets its descriptive meaning. But one moves to an explanatory understanding of *good* only to the degree to

[3]*Summa Theologica*, Pars Prima, q. 87, a. 4.
[4]'St Thomas and the Concrete Operabile', *Sciences Ecclesiastiques*, 1955–6; 'Complacency and Concern in the Writings of St Thomas', *Theological Studies* (20) 1959.
[5]Cf. B. Lonergan, *Insight*, 612–6.

which introspection of will has been successfully attempted. That successful attempt would reveal that there is a certain duality in the meaning of *good* corresponding to the two orientations of will, the orientation of complacency and the orientation of concern. That meaning involves two related sets of terms and relations. A parallel may help here. Just as insight into the diagram of a circle yields the definition of a circle which involves the concepts of line, point, etc., so insight into the experience of will yields such related terms. In the orientation of complacency those terms are basically the mutually defining *good* and *complacency*; in the concern orientation the basic terms are *concern, end, good*. Beyond this indication we do not intend to go. The expert will recognize here a focal source for the duality of St Thomas's treatment of the good. The initiate will acknowledge the parallel between the scientific and introspective treatment of the will and the scientific in other fields. As we remarked, the terms 'complacency' and 'concern' are technical. Insofar as the methodological education is successful, familiarity with such words will not lead to contempt for their scientific meaning and its relevance.

Our basic three levels may be appreciated in terms of the good, either as an object of complacency or as an object of concern. Consider an order of affairs, for example, a five-year economic plan which has been decided on and is going into operation. You will appreciate that this is a third level phenomenon. That level involves the realization of an order—economic, social etc.—that was considered to be good. That order or plan was perhaps one of several that arose from an understanding of the concrete situation and its possibilities: it was an answer to a What–question. Now you can appreciate without much difficulty that the answer to such a What–question is complex, is something more than butter and beef. It is not just a collection or a listing of particular goods. Each of us has the experience of the need of such goods, be it through hunger or thirst or, on a higher level, through the desire to understand. But the possible dynamic social structure is not any one good, but an ordering of goods—it is a good of order. It is of course at such a good of order that a party or government policy should aim, not yielding to the temptation either to promise merely particular goods or to promote some abstract deal. But since the mass of the people lean spontaneously towards the palpable, a policy of campaigning if not of government profitably leans similarly towards what appeals rather to the eye than to the ordering mind. Here we touch on that enormous field of discussion, human bias,[6] and we will pause for a moment on the related question of individual genuineness.

We may assume that most readers of this book are interested in genuineness on the level of intellectual development. That interest is the interest of a person, not of a pure intelligence and so it is multiply conditioned in its concrete pursuit. The focal element in that interest is the drive of wonder native to all men, but that focal element is meshed with degrees of willingness and the complexity of the psyche. We have said nothing so far about the psychic dimensions of human development; we have said nothing, indeed, about development at all. Yet we may appeal to the reader's general familiarity with human development to assert that genuineness is linked with sustained human development, and that the focus of that development lies in the intelligence. Implicitly our discussion of metaethics lays stress on the central role of intelligence in human doing, on the spontaneous demand within the person for consistency between his knowing and his doing. That stress is related to an opposite tendency which would leave a chasm between knowledge and love, or between truth and ethical imperatives. It would, too, undercut the apparent ultimacy of such categories as egoism and altruism. It is intelligence and reasonableness that assume

[6]B. Lonergan, *Insight*, especially 191–206; 218–42.

the ultimate position. Intelligence reveals to man a real order of things which places himself and his neighbour on a par within that order. It is to intelligence he must look if he seeks the renewal and development of that order. But if he is not to be continually harassed in that seeking by the biases of his group, the burdens of his psyche and the biological extroversion which he shares with the animals, then he must come to grips with the nature of the objectivity yielded by his intelligence. True, the biases and burdens of the human situation are challenged by faith and grace, and, less adequately, by the demands of fellow-feeling and intersubjectivity. But, just as the biases reach for theoretic expression, so their challenging calls for a movement into the theoretic. Contemporary human development requires that component which will reveal what is meant by objective human knowing. Without the genuineness that would reach for a knowing of knowing, we will remain victims of the eloquent nescience of ourselves and others, and our efforts at development will be continually bedeviled by one short term policy after another.

It is quite true that objective knowing is not yet authentic human living; but without objective knowing there is no authentic living; for one knows objectively just insofar as one is neither unperceptive, nor stupid, nor silly; and one does not live authentically inasmuch as one is either unperceptive or stupid or silly.

It is quite true that the subject communicates not by saying what he knows but by showing what he is, and it is no less true that subjects are confronted with themselves more effectively by being confronted with others than by solitary introspection. But such facts by themselves only ground a technique for managing people; and managing people is not treating them as persons. To treat them as persons one must know and one must invite them to know. A real exclusion of objective knowing, so far from promoting, only destroys personalist values.

It is quite true that concern for subjectivity promotes as much objective knowing as men commonly feel ready to absorb. Authentic living includes objective knowing, and far more eagerly do human beings strive for the whole than for the part. None the less it remains that the authentic living of anyone reading this paper, though it must start at home, cannot remain within the horizons of the home, the workshop, the village. We are citizens of our countries, men of the twentieth century, members of the universal church. If any authenticity we achieve is to radiate out into our troubled world, we need much more objective knowing than men commonly feel ready to absorb.[7]

[7]B. Lonergan, *Collection*, 238-9.

8

Collaboration in Truth

MOST people, perhaps, listen to the weather forecast on radio or television merely because, like the advertisements on T.V. it is interjected between more interesting items. It is listened to with varying degrees of attention and of scepticism. Some scarcely attend to it at all; others are fascinated by a mumbo jumbo about pressure and depressions; still others are sufficiently informed to follow the bulletin intelligently. The scepticism of some extends to considering the reverse of the forecast as nearer the truth; not a few regard it as little more reliable than putting a wet finger in the air or noting the colour of the evening sky; and there are those who concede that the morrow's weather will probably follow the pattern indicated. Now while all the elements and attitudes in the above situation are relevant to the present discussion, we will concentrate first only on some main points.

Obviously any listener and the weatherman are in different positions with regard to knowledge of the morrow's weather. Let us suppose for the moment that the weatherman who made out the report had at his disposal all the required instruments and that he made both observations and calculations himself. That being the case, in coming to his conclusions about the future weather he depended only on his own experience and observations and on his own scientific knowledge. He himself considered all the relevant factors, weighed the evidence and intelligently arrived at the present forecast. Coming thus to an intelligent conclusion includes appreciating just how certain the conclusion is. So the weatherman appreciates that he is not infallible, that the forecast enjoys a degree of probability, that its fulfilment depends on various complex conditions. Consider now the man who listens intelligently to the forecast and reasonably accepts it. No more than the weatherman does he take it to be infallible: accepting it intelligently he accepts it with a degree of certainty similar to the certainty of the weatherman, for he accepts both the scientific effort and its limitations. Ultimately then, the weatherman and the listener are informed about tomorrow's weather, yet differently so. I will denote that difference here by saying that whereas the weatherman knows, the listener in question believes. But let this not seem a predetermining of the issue by a choice of the use of the word 'belief'. The present article is not a prolonged dictionary definition. We are not listing the uses of the word 'belief'. We are trying to generate some understanding of the experience which we call believing. We take the listener's acceptance of the weather forecast as an instance of that experience. Some may object that this does not square with their notion of belief: let us bypass this objection conveniently by saying that we could have labelled the listener's experience with some other word but have opted for this word already used for a variety of human experiences. That much being clear we may return to our task. We say that what the weatherman knows, the listener believes. Furthermore we will keep rigidly to this terminology. We will use the word 'know' only when the knower himself examines the relevant facts, rightly understands what must be understood in the particular case, and intelligently concludes with true judgement. When this is not the case, as with the listener, we use the word 'believe'. By way of illustration let us note that many readers may not know that Ireland is an island, but certainly they all believe it is. Again for most of our readers the circulation of the blood is a matter of belief. Briefly we may say that whereas knowledge is immanently generated, belief is the acceptance of reliably communicated knowledge.

Before going on to analyse the experience we have called belief, let us face a more general question: why is there such a thing as belief? Clearly belief can be said to meet a real need. So one may listen to the weather forecast precisely because the activities of the morrow are to be determined by it. One needs information about the coming weather in order to act and since personal investigation is out of the question, one is willing to rely on the experience, understanding and judgement of others for this information. More generally, belief is part of all successful human collaboration, and collaboration is essential to human progress. Consider, for example, the ordinary occurrences during work on a building site. The crane operator does not know that the load is ready for lifting: he relies on the knowledge of the man who signals him. The bricklayer raises no questions about the stress and strain in the walls; more remotely, the engineer does not check the logarithm tables or slide rule at his disposal; and so on. Without this collaboration, which in every link includes belief, work on a building site would be a riot of individualism, fragmented into eccentric investigations into elementary problems, and the labour could scarcely be expected to yield us much more than a complex of stone igloos. And clearly what holds for a building holds much more for the building of a civilization.

The need for belief, however, goes deeper than the requirements of immediate action and successful cooperation. The continued labours of scientists bear witness to the unlimited desire of man for knowledge. Now no one man can know everything about everything. Further, no man can afford to begin at the beginning, nor can he investigate all he presupposes, nor indeed can he alone adequately verify the theories he evolves. Basic to the methodology of advancing science, and so obvious as not to be adverted to, is that no man confines his assents to his personal experience, understanding and judgement. The advance of human science is a matter of a collaboration which extends from nation to nation, from generation to generation. And the only alternative to that collaboration is a primitive ignorance. The collaboration, and the belief which it involves, even if not acknowledged in so many words, none the less exist and multiply continually. No mathematician nowadays masters all the branches of his trade; experimental scientists rely on the reports of colleagues, of predecessors and of the mathematicians; technologists do not take time out to check tables of function. No doubt it is a fact that any of these men might settle down to understand and check personally what their work presupposes. Yet it is no less a fact that they do not do this. Moreover such a successful check is in fact impossible. Human science is so radically a collective business that no scientist can have immanently generated knowledge of the really significant: for the significant evidence for any theory is precisely the common testimony of scientists, past and present, to the verification of the theory in their respective investigations, and this is evidence not for science but for belief.

Returning to our initial weather-forecasting example, we find that both the needs mentioned, the need to do and the more fundamental need to know, are illustrated by it. For, besides the need for information about the morrow's weather on the part of the particular listener, there is, it is hoped, the scientific satisfaction of the weatherman in adequately forecasting. Again it should be clear that if we presupposed that the weatherman carried out personally the necessary observations and calculations, we did so only for argument's sake. Indeed, even if only one station were necessary and all the instruments to hand, the weatherman has no personal guarantee that the instruments read true.

We have distinguished adequately between knowledge and belief. Still to separate the two in an individual mind is quite another thing: for the individual's mind is a complex network of knowledge and belief woven together inextricably over the years. Our present concern, however, is to distinguish the two by definition, and since one cannot distinguish by definition unless one can define, and one cannot define intelligently unless one understands, our first task is to generate some understanding of the nature of belief. The nature of knowledge has already been intimated.

Clearly both knowledge and belief are ways of coming to truth. In the first case one is relying on one's own understanding in the second case one is relying on the understanding of another. The second way of coming to truth is basically possible because of the first. For, when you reach knowledge of the truth, it is not just truth for you, a subjective truth. The truth you reach is in some way independent of you, and it is that independence that makes it detachable, communicable. So even if you have not the opportunity to investigate the grounds for a particular truth, when you have reached that truth you know that it is no less true for us. In brief, true judgement is not conditioned by the subject who reaches it. It is unconditioned in a radical fashion. For, whenever you make a true judgement you do so precisely because you have understood the situation, weighed the evidence and intelligently grasped that the conditions for the truth of this judgement are fulfilled, that the prospective judgement is unconditioned. This analysis may seem remote from our everyday experience of true judgement, yet our reflections have revealed that the above process occurs in all true judgements. As we have seen, it is more easily appreciated if one considers the complex evidence of a criminal trial and the consequent judgement on guilt. But it is also present in the everyday judgement. So, for example, someone may ask you at table, 'Is your tea cold?' Before you investigate you do not judge, you do not know. You seek evidence by sight, touch or taste, or merely recall that the tea was poured ten minutes ago. You grasp the sufficiency of the evidence, you grasp as unconditioned the prospective judgement, 'My tea is cold'. The sufficiency of evidence of course varies with circumstances: thus to frosty hands the tea may feel uncomfortably hot. However, what exactly is sufficient evidence in a given instance is a matter, not of rule, but of intelligent reflection. And when you eventually state, 'The tea is cold' you mean not just that it is cold for you, but that, simply, it is cold. Furthermore the statement is accepted as such by the original questioner: he intelligently believes that the tea is cold. And to the details of that intelligent acceptance we now turn. In order to appreciate these details one must necessarily proceed by examples in one's own experience of believing, such as the acceptance of a table of logarithms as true, or of the news report on the radio, or of the existence of atoms. Only thus will the basic steps involved in the process of coming to a belief become gradually clear to the reader.

First of all, coming to believe a given truth involves a complex of personal judgements prior to the particular act of belief. They may be prior as a habitual pattern of thinking and living. This type of prior judgement we have already touched on when we considered the role of belief in human living: whether we admit it or not, we already act on the conviction that belief in general is of value, that it is of value both to communicate to others the truths one has reached and to accept from others the truths they have reached. But besides this background of judgements on belief in general, there is in the case of any given proposition a more particular set of preliminary judgements concerning the accuracy of the communication from the original source of the truth, and the reliability of the source itself. It is evident from our discussion of truth that there is such a source: if there is a particular proposition which is proposed as true, that proposition cannot be belief for everyone, since belief is a secondary way of possessing truth. The particular proposition must be, not belief, but knowledge, for someone. Now one might well reach the preliminary judgements on the reliability of the source by seeking out that source. But it is well to note that even if one is fortunate enough to have a personal interview with the original knower, one is looking for evidence not for the particular proposition, but for belief. Thus one might interview a mathematician in order to see what sort of creature he is as a preliminary to believing his table of logarithms. But to ask him to provide evidence that the logarithm of one is zero is another matter, for one would then be seeking knowledge, not grounds for belief. This example merely serves to stress that the preliminary judgements are concerned with the evidence for belief in a particular truth, not with the evidence for the truth. For reaching these preliminary judgements there can be no general rule, beyond the rule of being alert, wide awake, critically reflective. So one may rely on personal knowledge of another's character, and one may advert to motives, to ability, to opportunity to deceive, to the check of scientific progress, to the exposing power of historical research, etc. In this way one moves from a basic conviction that, in general, belief is a human good to a judgement on the good of this particular belief. More accurately, the preliminary judgements lead one to grasp as unconditioned the value of deciding to believe this particular proposition, and this grasp finds its expression in a corresponding judgement of value. This judgement of value calls for a comment. The value in question is precisely the value of the personal possession of the particular truth. If this notion of value is to take on meaning for the reader he must advert to truths in his own experience which have such a quality. No doubt it is of value to the engineer to accept the table of logarithms if he is to get on with his job. No doubt it is of value to a theoretical physicist to accept the experimentalist's conclusions regarding atoms. No doubt more people than the newspaper reporter consider it of value to accept radio communications. Still, none of these examples may carry much weight for a given reader. Atoms and logarithm tables may mean little to you, and while you do actually believe the radio news, the effort to isolate the preliminary judgements of value in this case may be too much for you. So it is up to the individual reader to seek out and exploit such occurrences of belief as illustrate best for him the various elements of the process of belief which we touch on. The point requires emphasis because there is the all too human tendency merely to read and merely to remember an explanation, to be able to talk with ease about it and repeat it accurately, without ever facing the labour of understanding. The object of our reflection should be not just to remember an explanation, not even to understand an explanation (for what does this mean?) but to understand an experience, a personal experience, the experience of believing. With this important aside dominating, it is hoped, our attitude of mind, let us return to the task.

We noted that the preliminary judgements lead to a certain appreciation of the worth of any particular belief, and that this appreciation finds its expression in a judgement on the value of deciding to believe the particular proposition. From this appreciation, or intelligent grasp, the judgement necessarily follows, and if in fact we make this judgement then we cannot both be reasonable and fail to decide to believe. And from that decision there follows naturally the act of belief. There is, one might say, a clear follow-through from grasp of value to belief: to drag out the metaphor, at the bottom of the swing occurs the judgement of value, the swing naturally continues to a reasonable responsible belief, yet the whole movement depends on the downswing which ends in a grasp of the value of deciding to believe. This grasp of the sufficiency of the evidence for the judgement of value is clearly the key act in the process. The preliminary judgements lead to it; the sequence of other acts follow from it. That grasp is had insofar as one intelligently appreciates the general value of belief, the particular relevance of the given proposition, the accuracy of the communication from the source and the reliability of the source. It is not a matter of listing premises, of deducing conclusions or constructing syllogisms. No doubt these may help towards it: but there is no alternative to the intelligent and critical reflection on the sufficiency of the accumulated evidence for the belief. Finally, as we have indicated earlier, human certainty is a human thing which admits of a spectrum of degrees all falling below absolute certainty. Absolute certainty occurs only when literally everything that is in any way relevant is completely understood, and that understanding is not human but divine.

While we distinguished the judgement, the decision and the assent which are the act of believing, these three form a tight sequence following the basic grasp of value. Let us consider first the judgement of value. It resembles any other judgement that we make, for all reasonable judgements follow from an intelligent grasp of the evidence for them. So, for example, the occulist does not judge that a person needs glasses without testing his eyes and appreciating the sufficiency of these tests. Like any other judgement too, the judgement of value can be false if the preliminary investigation is inadequate or biased or influenced by other desires. It differs however from factual and theoretical judgements, in that it is a judgement of value, and the particular value in question is the good of possessing a particular truth.

The decision that follows the judgement of value, like any other decision, is free and responsible. Like any other decision it is reasonable and good if the prior judgement is honest, favourable and correct. Like any other decision, it depends on the intelligent grasp of a possible course of action. But the course of action envisaged in taking this particular decision is not an external activity, but the internal act of assent to the particular proposition.

Lastly, there is the crowning act of believing. By it the particular truth in question is accepted as true for you. The act by which you accept that truth is similar to any other act of judgement; for in any act of judgement one affirms or denies a certain proposition to be true with the simple Yes or No of reason. However, while in a judgement which is knowledge, what moves us to it is our own grasp of the evidence for it, in a judgement which is an act of belief we are moved also by the decision to take advantage of a particular human collaboration in the pursuit of truth.

More light will be thrown on the nature of belief when we pass on to discuss that particular instance of belief which is divine faith. Before moving on to that, however, let us consider some additional relevant, though scattered points.

An adequate treatment of belief should certainly include some account of mistaken belief. Clearly one can say that mistaken belief occurs because the process of coming to genuine belief, described above, has not been faithfully carried out. Yet to account for mistaken belief would require that one advance the reasons for this failure, and this would take us too far afield. Suffice it to note that the likelihood of mistaken belief, indeed of mistaken science, increases as the object of the belief or science involves man more intimately. One need only compare, say, the serenity of mathematics with the turbulence of the history of religions.

If there is mistaken belief, there is also the problem of its elimination. While faithfulness to the demands of the process of coming to genuine belief can exclude mistaken belief, this does not imply that to eliminate one's mistaken beliefs one must suspend all one's beliefs and settle down to a process of reconstruction. One would attempt such a process only if one were ignorant both of the nature of belief and of the manner in which belief is indistinguishably and extensively built into one's personal store of truth. Instead of undertaking such a fruitless and endless investigation of beliefs which are true, or probably so, one is altogether better employed in seeking out and investigating one single mistaken belief. For, in thus seeking one mistaken belief, one has the advantage of looking for the weakest link in one's own private network of truth, and if one is honest in pursuing that mistaken belief to its source in oneself, one is liable to expose other mistaken beliefs at their roots.

Besides mistaken belief there is disbelief. For example, a shift of the negative in the statement of mistaken belief, 'I believe that Caesar was not stabbed,' changes it into a statement of disbelief, 'I do not believe that Caesar was stabbed'. In this latter statement, however, there is an ambiguity that should not be missed. The initial 'I do not believe' may mean that one believes the opposite, and then the statement is equivalent to the first statement of mistaken belief. But it may also mean 'I neither believe nor disbelieve': it can thus mean that no investigation has been carried out, that I have neither interest nor evidence in the matter of Caesar's misfortunes. As distinct from the first possibility, that of positive disbelief, this is negative disbelief. Whereas negative disbelief requires no effort, positive disbelief, no less than belief itself, requires—if it is to be reasonable—that the same process of preliminary judgements, etc. be carried out in arriving at it. The above ambiguity obviously becomes more interesting with such a statement as 'I do not believe that God exists'. Taken in the negative sense this simply means that I have no interest in investigating the evidence for such a belief—in practice indeed it may mean that the superficial inconvenience of such a belief deters me from investigation. In the positive sense, the statement means that I have pursued the usual process of investigation, and have solid grounds for my unbelief. And since the latter solid grounds do not exist, such positive disbelief, though it may have psychic conditions, is lacking in reasonableness.

Again, one can be in, or move into, a state of doubt about one's beliefs or disbeliefs. Here it is important to note that like any state of mind, doubt is reasonable only insofar as there are reasonable grounds for it. Like any judgement, a judgement of doubt such as 'I doubt whether Caesar was stabbed' or 'I doubt whether I believe that Caesar was stabbed' requires personal grasp of sufficient evidence for it. This point is of vital importance when the statement in question is 'I doubt my faith': either such doubt is founded on genuine evidence personally and intelligently grasped, or it is not. And if it is not, as in fact it cannot be, then it is unreasonable, springing from one of the many influences that sway human intelligence from its goal.

Finally, one can believe something yet still raise questions about that belief. Such questions may spring from a desire to replace belief by knowledge: so, for example, one might undertake a trip around Ireland in order to know, and not merely believe, that it is an island. However, such a desire cannot always be satisfied: so, for example, even if one should hunt out one's sponsors and examine the parish register one can never know whether one is baptized or not; one must believe it. More usually, questions about a belief arise from the natural human desire to understand. So, for example, one may wish simply to understand Newton's theory of gravitation, and at the same time be in no way bothered about the degree to which it is verified. One remains thus in the state of believing that it is a good approximation, yet one advances towards an understanding of how the theory hangs together. Most evidently in the case of divine faith human wonder may raise questions of the latter type. These questions may concern what we believe or how we believe or the nature of the evidence for faith. Such questions, and the underlying desire, can indeed be distorted so as to lead, for example, to a state of doubt as described above. But insofar as human wonder about divine faith does not suffer distortion, it raises no question of certainty—for by faith one is already certain. Moreover, that wonder knows no limits. It moves a man to seek an understanding of his faith in a search which can be satisfied ultimately only by the vision of God.

It is time perhaps that we discussed in more detail the particular belief which is faith. Just as we found that belief in general was essential to the collaboration of men in human progress, in human knowing and human living, so we will find that faith is essential to the collaboration of men and God in that same human progress. No doubt the ordinary believer may never advert to the fact that his faith incorporates him into such a collaboration; for it is one thing to have faith, another thing to understand what having faith means. Pilate had expressed many truths in his life before he raised the question. 'What is truth?' In similar fashion, the Catholic's human wonder may only gradually lead him to raise the question, 'What is faith?' Our efforts here are directed towards answering that single question in such a way as to reveal the parallel between belief and faith and the manner in which the inadequacies of human collaboration give rise to problems which are met by a more-than-human collaboration.

Earlier we discussed the need for collaboration if men were to advance towards fuller human living, and the role of belief in that collaboration. Yet while the necessary collaboration is a substantial fact, it is no less a fact that it is not sufficient. For besides collaboration there is conflict, besides truth there is also falsehood, besides benevolence there is hate, besides human goodness there is human wickedness, besides human progress there is human decline. On the level of the group that failure in collaboration occurs between nation and nation, between class and class, and on the level of the individual there is the failure to be reasonable in behaviour, failure to identify the genuine goal of human desire. Moreover, the inadequacy can be met neither on group nor on individual level. For by nature man's living is prior to his understanding of how to live. To come to completely adequate knowledge of truths by which to live reasonably would require more than one human life, and meanwhile that life must be lived. And even if knowledge were not lacking, what guarantee is there that it would govern behaviour, that the individual would follow the demand of his reason? Furthermore, on the level of the group these difficulties are aggravated, not minimized. For on the level of the group there is the bias that fits theory to practice, that generates a multitude of philosophies in which truth can scarcely be distinguished, that continually inclines human living away from intelligence and reasonableness. In a word, there is the problem of evil, and there is no human solution to it.

Yet solution to it there is. Some are born into that solution, some find it after long years of search. But at all events a man cannot be true to his intelligence without both acknowledging the problem and raising the question of its solution. And in raising the question of a solution, from the nature of the problem he can anticipate certain characteristics of any solution. For the problem is a problem of human collaboration and progress at all times and in all places. If that problem is to be adequately met then the solution must have a like universality and permanence. Furthermore since the problem is a human one, the solution must meet it on the human level, it must be for men as they are, it must dovetail into the human situation yet transform it. That transformation must affect human knowing and human willing, for it is there that the problem has its roots. And since the range of human willing and human hope is limited to the truths that man possesses, the transformation at its most basic level must consist in a permanent supplementing of human truth.

Now we have seen that each man augments his personal store of truth by availing himself of the normal collaboration of men in its pursuit. Yet the existence of the problem of evil reveals the inadequacy of that collaboration, and an adequate solution, since it demands a supplementing of human truth, demands a higher collaboration, a collaboration not simply of men with one another but of men with God. Just as in belief man relies on the understanding of other men, so in faith man relies not merely on the understanding of other men, but on divine understanding. In the one case as in the other the group of collaborators share truth that is not belief but knowledge for at least one of that group. Again, just as the listener to the weather forecast would be surprised at our exposition of the presuppositions of his belief, so the Catholic would be surprised by the present exposition of the implicit presuppositions of his faith. Again, just as there are listeners for whom the weather forecast lacks interest because they intend spending the morrow in the shelter of home or office, so there are men for whom the Good News lacks relevance because they live in the shelter of an unthinking routine of petty pleasures and pains, or in the security of a pragmatist code of decency, of a humanism that is less than human. On the other hand a man is intelligent and reasonable to the extent that he grasps the existence of the prob- lem of evil, in himself and in general, and the inability of man to cope with it, to the extent that he recognizes and acknow- ledges that in human history divine wisdom and goodness has effected an adequate solution. To the general preliminary judgements he thus adds more particular judgements which enable him to grasp as unconditioned the value of deciding to assent to the truths of the higher collaboration. And, as in natural belief, from that grasp there springs necessarily the judgement of value, freely and responsibly the decision to be- lieve, and finally the act of faith itself. The object of that assent is the truths transmitted by the higher collaboration, and since that collaboration involves God as source and principal agent, the motive of the assent of faith will be the unlimited under- standing, goodness and power of God originating and preserving the collaboration. The certainty of that assent will be in some way absolute, for, just as an intelligent listener accepts the weather forecast as no more certain than the weatherman considers it to be, so the believer accepts the truths of faith as exactly as certain as the Source of faith knows them to be—and that knowledge is absolutely certain.

Our discussion of faith might end here. But we would like to recall some of the indications of chapter seven in this context. Consequent on faith there is man's basic affective response to faith, and because of the increasing popularity of what might be called a concerned existentialist attitude to life, a word about this basic Catholic attitude would not be out of place. We speak of a basic response to faith. We are not concerned here with man's continued active collaboration with God, his living by his faith. We are concerned with something prior and fundamental, an attitude which is in deep contrast with existentialism's stress on guilt, anxiety or despair. That basic response, consequent on the act of faith, should persist and grow with faith. We have already used the technical term 'complacency' in connection with such a response. Catholic belief is an acceptance of the truth about all that is, and complacency is the affective counterpart of that acceptance of all that is, as it is. That affective acceptance and the resulting attitude gives rise in the first instance not to action but to personal stability. It puts a person into harmony with reality as it is. It carries over into action; but complacency is a basic attitude of contemplation, the pilgrims foretaste of an eternal complacency in the vision of God.[1]

---

[1] The reader will find a helpful discussion of contemporary problems in faith in the closing chapters of the short work by F. E. Crowe S.J.: *A Time of Change: Guide for Perplexed Catholics*, Milwaukee 1968.

9

Man's Making of Man

' IT is not heredity that makes us human but always the content of a tradition. In heredity man possesses something virtually indestructible, in tradition something that may well get lost.'[1]

In our chapter on metaethics the social dimensions of the human subject's self-appropriation were only hinted at. When one begins the task of introspective analysis what comes first into focus is the subject as knower. So, in our opening chapters, the reader was led to discover himself as the inquiring subject. When we moved to consider the structure of the extension of knowing into doing we retained that focus: the centre of attention was the subject within himself, so to speak, rather than the subject within society or tradition. Now, against the background of our discussion of the extension of knowing to believing, we may move to the problem of man's collaboration, your collaboration, in the making of man.

In the course of our normal human development in society we gradually become not merely intellectual subjects but moral subjects. Jean Piaget has painstakingly documented the stages in this gradual growth.[2] He shows how the child's moral sense is developed and fostered by the society of both adults and peers. H. S. Sullivan[3] indicates how interwoven are the moral sense

[1]K. Jaspers, *The Origin and the Goal of History,* London 1953, 236.
[2]J. Piaget, *The Moral Judgement of the Child,* London 1932.
[3]H. S. Sullivan, *The Interpersonal Theory of Psychiatry,* New York 1953.

and the need for the esteem of others. But ultimately under-pinning that development and its generation of specific rules there is the common dynamic structure explicitated in chapter seven. The dynamic structure of action is merely structure, and just as we never merely know, but always know something, so we never merely do, but always do something. The doing something is multiply conditioned, by conditions of nerve, of habit, etc., but the conditioning that interests us here is the conditioning from society. We never merely do something, we act in the society where as a matter of fact we happen to be. Society, and the environment which is its expression, the embodiment of its meaning,[4] is the context of our activity and this fact prompts the question of the relation between insight, environment and society. There is no possibility here, of course, of anything more than a series of hints which may lead the reader to more accurate personal introspection.

When you attend to yourself in a concrete instance of practical inquiry, What is to be done?, Is it to be done?, two aspects of the activity may come to light. The first we have already mentioned: your action will in some way affect your society and will take place in society. The second aspect is that your society will present you with suggestions on how to act in certain circumstances. You will be confronted with laws, formulated or embodied, of behaviour. You will find yourself faced with a tradition. Of course, these two aspects are separated here for convenient analysis only. More accurately, you discover yourself as an ethical subject in a traditional society. Accordingly, the introspective analyst cannot avoid asking about the

[4]The significance of this phrase will come to light from the two following chapters. Let us note here, too, the relevance of the aesthetic, discussed in chapter eleven, and of satire and humour, as contributing to the transformation of society and as spontaneously critical of 'the slums of mind' (quoted on page xi above), and of 'the neon god' of the song, *Sounds of Silence* by Paul Simon. Spontaneous criticism, however, is not adequate. (Cf. *Insight*, pp. 237, 624–6).

nature and source of law, traditions, society. Let us, in our elementary consideration, pass over the subtler aspects of tradition and reflect only on that aspect associated with a commonly accepted meaning of law. The structure of such law can be expressed in the form of the major premise of an inference:

If A is the case, B is to be done.

Of course, in the oral or written code the law will not always, if ever, be expressed in that way, but this formulation has some pedagogical use. The inference expresses a link between certain conditions, A, and a mode of action, B. Grasping the link means grasping that B is the reasonable course of action in the circumstances A.

The structural identity between law and personal practical judgement may now be indicated. The personal practical judgement is expressed: B is to be done, because it is the reasonable course of action in the circumstances A, or, in other words,

Since A is the case, B is to be done.

Some readers, however, may supect that the law is an illegitimate generalization of the particular concrete practical judgement: for one thing, there is the problem of the uniqueness of the concrete situation. Eliminating this suspicion obviously requires a certain amount of introspective analysis. When you are confronted with a practical problem, you worry over and eventually devise a solution which you consider fits the circumstances. But the circumstances which you consider are not just any circumstances, or all circumstances, but only those which reveal themselves as relevant. So, if you are sitting at your desk wondering, say, whether or not to buy a new car, you do not consider relevant to your inquiry the fact that you are wearing a blue rather than a yellow tie. Similarly, you appreciate, or mean, that your eventual judgement would be the same if exactly the same relevant circumstances arose again. We do not say that exactly the same circumstances ever will arise again, but if they did then there would be no reason to change your

7

judgement, assuming that it is correct to begin with. Notice how this meaning makes possible the shift of judgement from:

Since A is the case, B is to be done,

to

If A is the case, B is to be done.

One may say, then, that the law is merely the formal expression of the original meaning.[5]

Now, since the law is structurally similar to personal judgement and indeed has a personal judgement as its source, it is subject to the same criticism as any judgement. But as well as this the law has the remoteness of an analytic principle.[6] Some of its terms may cease to have existential reference. Not only may case A be no longer possible, but the growth of human understanding and science which mediates such laws may transform the meaning of case A. As we indicated in the previous chapter, it is neither desirable nor possible for everyone to question all truths or all laws. Some laws and some truths must be believed. But when one faces a vocation of authentic criticism, inquiry becomes relevant. One may move in that inquiry to an investigation of the grounds for belief in the tradition, or to the larger investigation of the content of the tradition. In the chapter on metaethics we attempted to lead you to a self-critical position. Now the intrinsic movement of the inquiry leads beyond criticism of self, to criticism of self and society. It is not a matter, then, of abandoning tradition, or ignoring it merely because it is tradition. Whatever the tradition, implicitly it will claim to be reasonable. If it is, then it can stand scrutiny, and scrutiny may ensure that the tradition remain vital—and

[5]The reader will find it worth while to reflect on the laws of driving and their development, the variability of roads, vehicles, parking spaces etc., and his own intelligent operations as mediated by law and terminating in concrete behaviour.

[6]On analytic principles and propositions, cf. B. Lonergan, *Insight,* chapter 10, section 7.

we would note that a component of vitality is potentiality for development. We may note too that a tradition can become decadent not just because the original judgements were mistaken but rather perhaps because the meaning of the original judgements is lost or only the words remain. In a very exact sense, the spirit gives life, while the letter stultifies. In such a case scrutiny can lead, not to rejection, but to revitalization.

There is a further aspect to law which we mention merely in passing. The law can be expressed as the major premise of an inference, If A is the case, B is to be done. One responsibility of the critical, the authentically traditional, subject is to seek to grasp the link. Such a search requires the mediation of the relevant human sciences. A second responsibility regards the applicability of the law. The law is true for situation A as specified: but is A the case? This question, clearly, can be answered only by insight into the concrete situation.

We have, in a way, given a context for the remark of K. Jaspers which heads the chapter. Man possesses in tradition something that may well get lost. The consideration of law helps to reveal human society as at least in part a fabric of meanings, and tradition as a cooperation of meanings in a temporal dimension. Still, human meaning is not infallible, human progress is not a direct development, and so human history as well as being a cooperation and accumulation of meaning is also a clash of opposed meanings. Human history is a dialectic of ideas and their embodiment. It is a dialectic not merely of imperatives but, more fundamentally, of interpretations. For law, or any practical judgement, although it may be expressed as an imperative—B is to be done—is initially an interpretation. Thus the Marxian imperative concerning equal distribution of economic wealth is initially an interpretation of men in society, while the old doctrine of *laissez-faire*, before being a contrary imperative, is an opposed interpretation.

So we are driven back to inquire into the nature of social

order. An ambiguity appears here, for men are at once subject to and generative of law. Man is both ordered and orderer. Let us illustrate this point with an extremely simple example. Men are subject to fatigue: when they work too much and eat or sleep too little they collapse. Obviously that overtaxing of men may have its origin in a social order imposed by men, and such a social order is evidently doomed to failure. What is not taken into account may be on the level of biochemistry or physics, it may involve statistical or classical science, but the neglect may be nonetheless fatal to the order. A social order is an ordering of other orders and to be successful it must respect the routine of these orders. A social reformer who would institute equality must realize that political equality may not be enough. Thus the equality gained by the French Revolution was insufficient. It was an order of equality under which, as Anatole France remarked, rich and poor were equally entitled to sleep in a ditch.

Centrally a social order is an ordering of men by men, and the most evident problem here is that it is easier to attempt to manage people than to create an order in which they can develop as persons. Again, for limited ends, management is more efficient and simpler than the working out of an order which respects human freedom, which consequently allows for human aspirations, human feebleness, human error, human sin. Almost inevitably the reformer in power becomes the tyrant whether religious or political. Force, whether physical or moral, whether the more subtle exploitation of symbol or the less subtle exploitation of work-study, is always possible and will readily be availed of. Moreover, where production rather than people dominates the major premise, it is ever plausible. To manipulate people in the interest of oneself, one's group or one's country may demand little more than the rhetoric of persuasion.

The social order is an order of orders. So the economic order is not a development out of the blue but an attempt to employ the technology efficiently. The political order is not just any pattern but an effort to regulate the economy. Set out in this way the role of insight is revealed. The economic order is based on the technology yet the technology does not determine the economy. The possibilities of any technology are various and a particular economy is the implementation of only one of these possibilities. Still, the possibilities of any technology are not always obvious and so two limitations appear. The first and clear limitation is an inherent one: possibilities are many but not everything is possible. The second limitation is more significant and in our present context should not be entirely inevident: in order to implement any possibility, it must first be grasped as a possible object of rational choice from among other possibilities. For the most obvious possibility is not always or even frequently the best: so it is that the shift from classical to Keynesian economics is not so much a shift in the technology as a shift in meaning at the level of economic theory.

However, the underlying order does not remain static and besides development in the understanding of how to exploit the same technology, there is also the development of the technology itself. So there is a shift in the means of communication from waterways, to road, to railroads, to air. Again, not only are there new possibilities for transporting materials, but information can be relayed differently from letter, to telegraph, to telephone and television. Such technological development may run ahead of the economist or the politician's understanding of the profound changes that are being forced on the economy or the social structure by the new technology. Thus it happens that politicians may make their political decisions in a world of their own which no longer exists and appear blatantly immoral because, among other reasons, they are less apparently irrelevant and out of date. Thus—our example is illustrative, not theoretic—a ministry of transport might exhaust itself in supplying bigger and better roads for bigger and better cars, when the technology may have advanced, as we have noted, not only in locomotive communication but also in non-locomotive communication, and a modification of the notion of personal travel might leave sections of the concrete network obsolete.

The technology does not determine the economy and the polity, but it does set limits. A technology offers a range of possibilities and a successful economic or political system falls within that range. When a technology changes, the range of possibilities shifts and last year's adequate policy may not fall within the new range. Politics is the art of the possible in a more profound sense than is commonly acknowledged.

A change in the technology is already a change in the many-levelled order that we name the social system. An advance in technology is the product of a new insight but the insight that gives rise to the new technique may not encompass the consequences of the invention. It is one thing to invent the telephone. It is quite another to understand how the use of the telephone will or should affect the social system as a whole. Indeed it is common enough that an appliance is used and promoted without this understanding. As we have been indicating throughout the book, living precedes understanding living and it is easier to become familiar with ourselves and our artifacts than to understand ourselves and the remote significance of our artifacts. The fact that technology and inventions stay ahead of the understanding of their significance and consequences accounts for the fact that the economic and, perhaps more obviously, the political policy often runs out of date in a curious and ill-defined fashion. Furthermore, as McLuhan hints and others have remarked, the lag in understanding explains why a new invention is understood in terms of what it appears to replace. Print replaces writing and so it is assumed that print is exactly the same thing as writing only more efficient; the car replaces the horse and it is understood as a more efficient horse; the television is understood as an instant book; the telephone as

the same as talking face to face. The plain fact that an advance
in technology brings with it a new structuring of time and
space is overlooked. Of course, the different media do more
than this, but the structuring of time and space is basic. Technology in one of its aspects at least may be described as the
initial arrangement of time and space.[7] While it is not an ordering, apart from the economy and the polity, it evidently has not
the indeterminacy of a prime matter, a space-time continuum.
Its structured potentiality, underpinned by the dynamism of
invention, throws a strain on the layers of man's meaning
which inform it. So, as technology and technological skill advance, the need for the social scientist becomes ever more
urgent. At a certain level the pace of innovation in a particular
sphere is such that the required adaptations to the new technology occur more or less spontaneously, but the pace of
invention can so exceed the pace of spontaneous adaptation,
that adaptation can no longer be left to spontaneity: the discovery is made that intelligence requires the crutch of method
and so a new area of human science emerges.

This ever growing body of human sciences is both theoretical, in its concern with discovering what is the case, and
practical, in facing the question, What is to be done? But in
neither case can these sciences be considered adequate if they
are conceived as strangely positive, non-normative. To talk of
non-normative human sciences is to talk of pseudo-science
which turns a blind eye on a central feature of its data. Moreover, that central feature, the sphere of human understanding
and doing, is not something as plain as the positive integers. In
the concrete it is generative of a surd. If the surd and its source
are real then they are to be understood, and the surd is to be
understood in a way which has the peculiarities of inverse
insight, the entire understanding being intrinsic to the science

[7]One might reflect on this in the context of B. Lonergan, *Insight,* 172, and
its background.

as theoretic. Moreover, as that theoretic is theoretic of the actual order, there is no great chasm between the theoretic and the facing of the question, What is to be done? From another aspect we may note that the transition is not one from empirical or positive science to normative or practical science but from the complacent stance of the theoretician to the orientation of concern. To put the same point again, the question, What is to be done?, is not a question to be raised when inquiry into the economy and the polity has been concluded in some factual fashion. It is anticipated in this inquiry, for this inquiry must avail of developmental and dialectic method and intrinsic to its results is an understanding of intelligible and intelligent orientation. Again, the focal norm of doing is reasonableness, and what is reasonable cannot be determined in advance but only in the actual context of the problem. But that actual determination is mediated by, or against the background of, the adequate theoretic understanding of the many-levelled system, and the question of reasonableness is not an afterthought to that understanding. The human scientist must learn to distinguish between progress and decline, must learn to distinguish intelligently between the structure of an environment where human development is possible in its full range and that of an environment which operates like an efficient machine where limited ends are easily achieved. Nor is it as easy to distinguish between these two as might at first be thought.

Present trends in education are revealing of this, for thinking and learning, which, as we have seen, are apparently inefficient procedures, are ousted in favour of the more obviously efficient purveying of information.

Without its technicians, technology would turn into a museum piece; but with technicians only, or with men whose only interest is the immediately practical, the vast and complex technology, economy and polity become a worthless stage, 'the actors in the drama of living become stage-hands, the setting is magnificent; the lighting superb; the costumes gorgeous but there is no play.'[8]

We have, you may have noticed, come back once again to the central problem raised in chapter one, to the question of the control of meaning and of the emergence of meaning. The need for self-attentive methodology is now seen in a new context. As it is central to the subject's understanding of himself, so it is central to the subject's understanding of society and other selves. The same point may be made from another angle. While understanding understanding may be considered as somewhat extrinsic to the science of physics, it is very definitely intrinsic to an understanding of man.

You may, however, have slipped somewhat from the self-attentive stance as you read this chapter. You may have fallen into the trap of thinking that we were talking about society rather than about yourself. But our concern was, as usual, introspective. Our talk was indeed directed to your reorganization of your common sense and science.[9] We were trying to reveal some of the aspects of the demand mentioned in our chapter on metaethics: authentic living cannot remain within the confines of the home and 'if any authenticity is to radiate out into our troubled world, we need much more objective knowing than men feel ready to absorb'.[10] So far we have outlined some areas where such objective knowing is required but more significantly for our purpose we have gradually led you to discover the guiding practical question which emerges once you have grasped the present time as the possibility of the future. A consideration of the question, What is to be done?, has revealed the general structure of the solution, but it has also revealed a problem. If there are some who would work towards a society in which human freedom and human devel-

---

[8]B. Lonergan, *Insight*, 237.
[9]B. Lonergan, *Insight*, 388-9.
[10]B. Lonergan, *Collection*, 239.

opment are possible, there are others who for their own ends would promote a society where they would prosper while others would lose or gain indifferently in function of what best suited the organiser's interests. The demands of intelligence are stifled and intelligence becomes the servant of other purposes. The reader should not try to search for historical examples of this bias. There are examples in history. They are many, obvious and, for our present purpose, almost irrelevant. Your problem is to discover facets of bias in yourself. Needless to say, bias is not as obvious as our extreme example suggests. It works covertly, questions that should arise do not arise, problems that should be faced are not faced, solutions that should be examined are embraced with enthusiasm because they suit or are rejected with vigour because they do not; accepted solutions are bolstered up with specious reasons, while the contrary reasons are either forgotten or ridiculed; rejected solutions are vilified and the integrity or intelligence of their proponents is questioned; a solution is accepted and any murmurs against it, any questions that arise, are muffled or greeted with a look of incomprehension or pity; and so on.

What is true of the individual can be true of the group. Any group in a society obtains certain benefits and suffers some hardships. Naturally, group feeling is to enlarge the benefits and reduce the hardships, even at the expense of other members of the wider community. Of course the bias is not so crudely manifested, nor need it be clearly appreciated. It acts as before: questions are inhibited, problems are ignored, solutions are hailed or jeered at with uneasiness or even a passion that betrays the flight from reason.

Bias has the same general character throughout. It is the gradual shift away from questioning. Questioning is the key to human intellectual development, but sometimes questions seem to point to unacceptable solutions, and so the question is pushed aside. It is easy enough to forget the question. You can go to the pictures, to a play, to the pub. Anywhere. The quality of the distraction is of little consequence: whether Nero ate or slept or played the violin is not of great moment. The forgetfulness of the question, the erection of a mode of living in which awkward questions will not easily arise is not too difficult for the man of average intelligence. It is the fall into everyday inauthenticity to which Heidegger frequently refers. In our terms, it is the gradual but relentless contraction of horizon. If the contraction is merely individual, then the society has merely one more inauthentic member. If the contraction becomes pervasive throughout the society, then wise men read the signs of the times and wait for the close of another era, for the content of the tradition is already lost.

10

Symbols and Syllogisms

'A FAMILIARITY with the elements of logic can be obtained by
a very modest effort in a very short time. Until one has made
notable progress in cognitional analysis, one is constantly tempted to mistake the rules of logic for the laws of thought.'[1]

By now the reader is used to our protestations of limited
treatment. Here more than elsewhere our treatment will be
sketchy. Self-attentive methodology opens up the possibility of
a radical renovation of logic and its foundations. A context for
that renovation is given by Helmut Stoffer in his discussion of
six types of logic: [1] Plane, [2] Dialectic, [3] Existential, [4]
Magical, [5] Mystical, [6] Hermeneutical.[2] Indications of direction in that renovation have been given by the authors,[3] the
source of these being the works of Lonergan, where more
basic indications are available.

We will content ourselves here, at all events, with some
further pointers. Let us begin with a simple geometrical illustration. We recall again that our interest is methodological:
we ask the reader to attend to himself as well as to the geometry.
A first thing to note, of course, is that while we print the puzzle

[1]B. Lonergan, *Insight*, 573.
[2]'Die Modernen Ansätze zu einer Logik der Denkformen', *Zeit. Für Phil.
Forschung*, (10) 1956, 442–66, 601–21.
[3]G. Barden, 'The Symbolic Mentality', *Philosophical Studies*, (XV)
Maynooth 1966, 28–57; P. McShane, 'The Foundations of Mathematics'.
Modern Schoolman, (40) 1963, 373–87.

the reader will very spontaneously—we hope—reach for pen and paper and draw a diagram. Obviously this fits into our general theorem regarding the need for phantasms in order to understand. But now we wish to note the further point that some phantasms are better than others. This point will carry us much further than might be suspected at this stage: we may hint at this here by noting that as well as the seen logical symbol there is the affect-laden sight of a city.

At any rate in geometry it is quite clear that the written-out problem and even the written-out solution can be far less adequate than a suitable diagram from which, one might say, the solution stares one in the face. The solution written out is a symbolic expression of our understanding—we use the word 'symbol' in the mathematical sense, as an equivalent to sign, and not in the sense of affect-laden image. The print is a series of conventional signs of meaning, and it is at a remove from what is to be understood. At the other extreme there are such images as the drawn circle: when one is searching for the definition of a circle it is the roundness of the drawn circle that one concentrates on. Wonder is directly engaged with the object to be understood. Trying to understand the properties of parallel lines provides an illustration of a somewhat different type of image. One cannot draw or imagine indefinitely produced straight lines. In this instance one may say that the image is virtual, and the key to the use of such an image is the mediation or intervention of understanding: the lines are drawn a bit but thought of as indefinitely produced. Understanding can dominate the image even further, as with conventional language. We settle just what a given image is to stand for through the intervention of definition. So it is with the conventional meaning of the sight and sound of the English language. But before we say more about this settling of meaning and the judicious choice of image let us expose our puzzle in the conventional symbolism of print.

In a circle of, say unit radius, two diameters, perpendicular to each other, are drawn. From an arbitrary point P on the circumference two perpendiculars PR and PS are drawn to the two diameters. The problem is, what is the ratio of RS to the radius? You have now drawn the figure? Perhaps even solved easily the puzzle? Your reaction to the puzzle and your solution of it will depend very much on your habits of mathematics. If mathematics leave you cold, then you may find it hard enough to make a proper diagram much less solve the puzzle. If you are a mathematician then the solution is just too obvious. If you fall in between these two extremes then you may draw and mark and puzzle, even try trigonometry. Joining R and S will be an evident thing to do: but it may take a pedagogue to adequately dispose the phantasm by the drawing of another line. The line to draw is the line joining the centre to the point P, say OP. Eureka! With the insight emerges the solution, the relation between RS and the Radius.

Now note that the solution can be formulated or thrown into syllogistic form, and this will help you get some light on features of the syllogism which are often misrepresented. We have, therefore, the syllogism:

$$RS = OP$$
$$\text{and } OP = Radius,$$
$$\text{therefore } RS = Radius.$$

In this light we may note important characteristics of procedure. We started, not with two premises, but with the conclusion in the form

$$RS \; ? \; Radius$$

Our search, through diagram, was for a middle term, and the middle term was supplied as soon as one adverted to the significance of OP. Only then can the syllogism be constructed. To coin an expression for this constructing, let us say that the insight is crystallized into a syllogism. This does not mean of course that somehow the insight has been pinned down on a page. What has happened is that we have given the insight explicit symbolic expression. Giving all the relevant insights explicit symbolic expression is by no means always an easy thing to do, even when it can be done. Modern geometers have found fault with Euclid in this matter. There are insights involved in the Elements which are not explicitly acknowledged either in the axioms or in the theorems, yet which were not uncrystallizable. We may illustrate this neatly from a piece of Felix Klein's discussion of geometry.[4] We need not enter into the details of this problem. Roughly, it concerns (cf. page 96) drawing a line from $1'$ to $\frac{1}{2}$, across a triangle yOx. In the process he remarks '. . . the unique constructibility . . . of the point $\frac{1}{2}$ as the intersection of the x axis with the path curve from $1'$ . . . would be assured if we only knew that this path curve really cut the x axis. Of course, no one would doubt this, intuitively, but in the framework of our axiomatic deduction we need a special axiom, the so-called "betweenness axiom" for the plane. This axiom states that if a line enters a triangle through a side, it must leave it through another side—a trivial fact of our space perception which requires emphasis as such, because it is independent of the other axioms.'[5] 'If we omit this, as Euclid does, we cannot reach the ideal of a pure logical control of geometry. We must continually recur to the figure.'[6]

Let us note further that our simple puzzle and solution is a paradigm of how Euclid and company may well have proceeded in most of the Euclidean theorems. They did not proceed step by step down the page of the modern text-book, from the stated theorem, to the fully constructed diagram, to the step by step deduction beneath. One should note too the significance of this for the teaching of geometry. Too often the

[4] *Geometry*, Dover, 165.
[5] *Ibid.*. 165.
[6] *Ibid.*, 201.

pupils begin, not with the thrill of a puzzle but with the top of the page, and at most they get a vague line-by-line comprehension of the theorem. Memory is burdened, and examinations consist in filling out theorems—from the bottom and top of the page!—and passing over the riders.

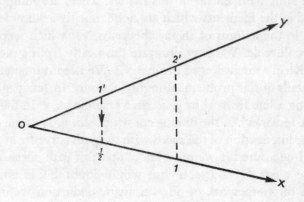

We may return now to a brief consideration of the simple symbolic expression of understanding which is the syllogism. We will distinguish here just two main types of syllogism and with them associate the two main types of proof. These two main types are related to the two main types of question which we discussed earlier.

Let us consider first the syllogism which is associated with the What–question. The syllogism given in connection with our simple problem was of this type, and it may be called the syllogism helping towards direct understanding. Now 'helping towards understanding' is precisely the role that this syllogism can play. This 'helping towards understanding' is related to what we mentioned earlier about the judicious choice of symbolism. The syllogism is so structured as to facilitate the understanding of the relevant relation. Much more of course could be said about the syllogism, but we wish to emphasize this one point: that the syllogism is not a mysterious replacement for understanding. Again one may look on the syllogism as a proof of the conclusion: but this can only mean that the structure facilitates a grasp of the implication of the conclusion in the premise. One might note too that such structures facilitate the checking, the Is–question, relating to that grasp: this could lead to a discussion of the question, among others, of consistency in wider areas, a larger study. At all events it should be evident to the reader that we have exemplified here one definite type of proof, one which occurs centrally on the level of the What–question. It is deductive proof, the proof normally associated with mathematics.

Besides deductive proof there is proof in the sense of verification. In this sense one can prove that the law of gravity holds, or that iron does not float in water. This sort of proof is centrally associated with the Is–question and it is reached by a reflective act of understanding which grasps sufficiency of evidence. Just as in the case of direct understanding, so here one can be helped to reach that grasp by syllogistic expression. We have indeed made use of such expression in chapter four, but there it fulfilled the more subtle function of helping the reader to grasp the grasp, so to speak.

'As has been seen already, the function of syllogistic expression is not to eliminate but to facilitate the occurrence of the reflective act of understanding. A parrot or an electronic computer can send forth signs in a syllogistic pattern; but neither can grasp the virtually unconditioned; and neither can be subjected to the rational necessity that results in a judgement.'[7]

We are emphasizing continually this single point. Furthermore, one can lay out the evidence, the case, symbolically, showing the links in such a way as to make it easy for a person to move to a grasp of the sufficiency of the evidence and the

[7]B. Lonergan, *Insight*, 710.

8

fulfilment of the conditions. But it is quite another thing for that person to grasp, or indeed to be willing to try to grasp. The horse may be brought to the water.

We leave to the reader the task of manufacturing syllogisms which are related to the Is–question. We would like to note however, that the process of coming to belief can also be helped in the same way. Consider for example the syllogism,

Whatever A tells me is credible, and to be believed by me,

A tells me X,

Therefore X is credible and to be believed by me.

As in all syllogisms of this type, the 'therefore' in the conclusion represents the possibility of a reflective act of understanding. As our chapter on the nature of belief indicated, the transition to the act of belief is not just a matter of reflective understanding: will and willingness are involved. But the same basic principle holds of 'suitable lay-out' of evidence, steps, links.

Let us go a little further into this question of suitable lay-out, judicious choice of signs, etc. It is a region of concern for pedagogues and advertisers, but our interest here, let us not forget, is a meta-interest. What is the significance of symbolism? First, symbolism is, in a certain sense, a 'lay-out', an objectification of mind. We have gone far enough now in cognitional analysis, perhaps, to appreciate that this does not mean that understanding has been pressed into a page, that truth has been made so independent of a particular mind that it exists without any mind. The objectification in question here is closely related to the suitability of the lay-out. Consider for example our illustration in chapter three of the taking of a square root. There we said that there was a technique by which the square root of a number could be arrived at. Any schoolboy would do it with a little practice, yet without understanding the Why of it all. The symbolism is suitable, the technique far from subtle. Try on the other hand getting the square root of the same number expressed in Roman numerals. Again, even if one understands the Why of the technique, still one takes the root without any effort of understanding, as something routine. Nor are logic and mathematics isolated instances of such procedure, of inbuilt implication and routine movement to result. You may think of the watchmaker with precise skill but perhaps no understanding of the Why of the watch, of balance-wheel and escapement, or you may consider the enormous development of modern technology. An interesting instance of the coupling of modern technology with adequate logical symbolism is provided by the computerizing of the famous *Principia Mathematica* of Whitehead and Russell:

> The author is interested in proving theorems with computing machines. In this connection he wrote three programmes for an IBM 704. The first programme provides a decision procedure for the propositional calculus which leads the machine to print out a proof or disproof according as the given proposition is a theorem or not. It was found that all theorems of the first five chapters of the *Principia Mathematica* were proved in 37 minutes, $\frac{12}{13}$ of the time being used for read-ins and print-outs. The second programme instructs the machine to form propositions of the propositional calculus and select non-trivial theorems. The author writes that the results were disappointing in so far as too few theorems were excluded as being trivial. The third programme is for the predicate calculus with equality. It is claimed that this programme can find and print out proofs for about 85% of the theorems in Chapters 5–10 of P.M. in about an hour.[8]

We may now turn back to consider the enormous develop-

---

[8]Steven Orey, in a review of Hao Wang's work reported in *IBM Journal of Research and Development* (4) 1960, 2–22; *Journal of Symbolic Logic* (30) 1965, 249.

ments of modern symbolic logic. In the light of the present discussion one should be in a better position to appreciate what is going on in this field.

One might consider mathematical logic as a study of deductive systems, a study which generates a series of hypotheses on the nature of deductive systems. Now, as any logician will tell you, such a study would scarcely be possible without the elaboration of a large set of symbols with definite rules of construction for complex expressions. In other words, the modern understanding of deduction depends on what is equivalent to a technological development on the level of sign. But one must be careful here to distinguish between the symbolism and the object of understanding. Consider, for example, the effort we made in chapter three to reach a definition of the ellipse. In reaching that definition we were helped by the diagram, the operations and such symbols as $AP + BP$. Generally in analytic geometry one 'leans on' both diagrams and symbolism, and anyone who has actually done analytic geometry will appreciate the value of the symbolism in the solution of problems, how at times it, as it were, takes over. At any rate, the object understood in that example was the ellipse, and what we reached was the definition of the ellipse—which, we recall, is unimaginable. The reader may notice a certain amount of ambiguity in the previous sentence. There are indeed two objects understood, but differently so, and it is helpful to introduce a suggestive technical distinction. We may speak of the imagined ellipse as the 'moving object' for intelligence, and of the definition of the ellipse as the 'terminal object'. Through this illustration it is perhaps easier to appreciate the statement that mathematical logic has as terminal object the definition of deductive system, this being understood in its broadest sense, involving thus the range of inverse-insight theorems like those discussed by J. Ladriere,[9] and n-valued logics. Here again we

[9]*Les Limitations Internes des Formalismes*, Paris 1957.

skip over interesting points of discussion such as the factual reference of such systems and the question of truth in logic. We stick rather to the central point of the chapter: the role of symbols in the control and generation of insight. Just as in analytic geometry, the symbolism in logic can carry one on, suggest changes, expose inadequacies. The expression of axiom systems in apt symbolism, for example, may be called virtual images: recall the similar cases of parallel lines and distinguish between the two types of virtuality.

Again, the same symbolic technique can play the role of 'moving object' in a series of different fields, 'isomorphic fields' as they are called. Here we no doubt have lost the general reader but the mathematician may recall such illustrations as lattice theory, or the associated power of implicit definition. Stefan Banach, in a paper which developed the basic notions of Banach spaces, puts the matter well: 'This present work has the object of establishing certain theorems that hold in several different branches of mathematics, which will be specified later. However, in order to avoid proving these theorems for each branch individually, which would be very wearisome, I have chosen a different way, which is this: I consider in a general way sets of elements for which I postulate certain properties. From these I deduce theorems and then I prove for each separate branch of mathematics that the postulates adopted are true.'[10]

We have stressed here the relation between the possibility of the investigation of the field of logical relations and the development of suitable symbolic techniques. We mentioned, in

[10]'Sur les operations dans les ensembles abstraits et leur applications aux equations integrals', *Fundamenta Mathematica*, (3) 1922, 134. The translation is by W. Sawyer in his *A Path to Modern Mathematics*, Penguin, 193. We may remark here on the significance of Sawyer's books as laying implicit stress on insight into phantasm. As well as his series of Pelican books, we note here his paperback *A Concrete Approach to Abstract Algebra*, San Francisco 1959.

passing, the region which deals with limitation theorems, a region which marks one type of limitation on symbolic expression. Thus, according to Church's thesis, 'recursive undecidibility is equivalent to effective undecidibility, i.e., non-existence of a mechanical decision procedure for theoremhood. The non-existence of such a mechanical procedure means that ingenuity is required for determining whether any given well-formed formula is a theorem.'[11] Various other limitations of symbolic expression are noted by Lonergan in his discussion of the limitations of the treatise.[12] Here we are concentrating on limitations on the level of mathematics and logic. We may note further that even in the strict derivation of conclusions of modern deductive systems, with fully formulated axioms and rules of inference, what Mendelson calls 'ingenuity' and Suppes calls 'intuition' or 'insight' is necessary. To quote an example from Suppes, '. . . to derive from the axioms what is known as the *right-hand cancellation law* . . . the crucial step is realizing what substitution in axiom [1] is appropriate . . . For with this insight goes the perception that $zoz^1 = e$ by virtue of axiom [3].[13]

There are then the casual insights which, as it were, step through the net of formulation. It is the business of formal logic of course to trap all that can be trapped: 'Its function is to make explicit all the essential elements whether they are obvious or not.'[14] That quotation serves to recall Lonergan's significant work, in the article cited, on the reduction to one general form of all valid forms of inference. Needless to say, to appreciate his discussion and conclusion you must be operating in the introspective mode. Otherwise you will be constantly puzzled about what he is at, you will wonder what all the fuss is about, and

[11]E. Mendelson, *Introduction to Mathematical Logic,* Princeton 1964, 151.
[12]B. Lonergan, *Insight,* 573–7.
[13]P. Suppes, *Introduction to Logic,* Princeton 1957, 106.
[14]B. Lonergan, 'The Form of Inference', *Collection,* 6.

you 'may miss the turning leading to an understanding of understanding.'[15] It is no easy matter to self-attend one's way understandingly through the article cited.

In this context we may note the discussion of W. Kneale and M. Kneale of Aristotle's neglect of the form of inference.[16] This neglect leads to an exaggeration of the opposition of the Aristotelian position and modern logic, the axiom systems of which so evidently involve formalization of the properties of inference.[17] Obviously there are other reasons for the opposition of Aristotelian and Scholastic logic to modern logic, but we note only this one, and the relevance of Lonergan's reduction to its removal. The problem is to reach an understanding of the roots of reasoning. We are not God, nor are we angels. Our understanding develops, reasoning is motion towards understanding, a motion involving the symbol. The simple hypothetical argument expresses the general form of that motion: 'Just as "so that" and "in order that" express the relations of efficient and final causality, so also "because", "although" and "if" are the special tools of reasoning man,'[18] and that motion 'comes to a term in the intuitive apprehension of a field of implications, interrelations.'[19]

A little Latin declension brings us from *inferre* to the illative sense of Newman, and a hint to the reader that the form of deductive inference which Lonergan uses in *Insight*[20] has a history and a significance that are far from evident at first sight. In this

[15]Cf. p. 28 above.

[16]*Development of Logic*, Oxford 1962, 96–100.

[17]Cf. for example E. Mendelson, *Introduction to Mathematical Logic;* the axiom system for propositional calculus, page 31, and first order theories, page 57.

[18]B. Lonergan, *op. cit.,* 4.

[19]B. Lonergan, *Verbum: Word and Idea in Aquinas,* 55. Cf. the index of this book under *syllogism, logic* and related topics.

[20]B. Lonergan, *Insight,* 280–1.

region of the Is–question we find, too, a further instance of the limitation of symbolisms.[21]

But we had best stop here if our discussion of symbols is not to go beyond the scope of the present short work. As we remarked, we had no aspirations towards complete treatment. We have no doubts, however, that a complete and renewed treatment of logic is required and made possible on the foundations of self-attention.[22]

---

[21]Cf. B. Lonergan, *Collection*, 5.
[22]Cf. the indications in *Insight*, especially 574, 576.

11

Symbols and Cities

'AT the opposite extreme from mathematical expression stands the great phenomenon of artistic expression, the symbolization of vital and emotional experience for which verbal discourse is peculiarly unsuited. Epistemologically this sort of symbolic presentation has hardly been touched.'[1]

In our last chapter we dealt with symbolism in the context of a very specialized field within the intellectual pattern. We swing now to the other extreme to touch on certain aspects of symbolism in the context of total living. Just as in our discussion of logic in the previous chapter, so here in our discussion of living we do not aim at complete summary coverage. We aim rather at orientating the reader to a proper approach to the self-attentive methodology of this sphere, in particular the sphere of the arts. With that aim we associate the aim expressed somewhat as follows by Lonergan in a talk on art during a seminar on education: 'What I want to communicate in this talk on art is the notion that art is relevant to concrete living, that it is an exploration of the potentialities of concrete living, that it is extremely important in our age when philosophers for at least two centuries, through doctrines on economics, politics

---

[1]Susanne Langer, *Mind: An Essay on Human Feeling*, I, Baltimore 1967, 80. This book is henceforth referred to as Langer, 1967.

and education, have been trying to remake man and have done not a little to make human life unlivable.'

According to Stephen Ullman, emotive overtones in language are almost unavoidable except in treatises on logic and mathematics.[2] We move here then from the rare and exceptional sphere of the symbol as sign to the sphere where symbol is to be taken to mean affect-laden image.

The methodology of art within the works of Lonergan may be said to be largely a transformation of that of Susanne Langer.[3] That transformation can be missed in various ways which the attentive reader might possibly identify for himself immediately. In the first place, either one pursues this investigation through the well-defined scientific method of introspection or one does not, and if one does not then one is liable to be tied to a refined description if not to a mere use of words. In the second place, the investigation and its conclusions must be consistently taken in the context of the structured critical realism dealt with in the earlier chapters. The real is still, let us recall, what is to be reached by correct understanding. It is far from easy to pursue a discussion of art within that critical horizon. There is a constant gravitation towards taking the discussion to the obvious 'realistic' level of the already-out-there-now. Thus we might write here, with Susanne Langer, of the piano as a living presence in a room.[4] We write thus, meaning the real piano in the real room and its artistic import. But perhaps you find that spontaneously you think about the large brown object out there in the corner? You note that we are back at the problem of the Bridge of Asses of chapter five. There is an interesting relation between our Asses' Bridge and what Langer holds to be the Asses' Bridge of art theory.[5] The

[2] *The Principles of Semantics*, 1963, 13.
[3] Especially contained in *Feeling and Form*, London 1953, to be referred to below as Langer, 1953.
[4] Langer, 1953, 100, footnote.
[5] Langer, 1967, 97, footnote.

latter Asses' Bridge involved considering representation as nothing more than a device: indeed, 'The heavy leaning on the fruits of exact observation as symbols is merely one technique, one method of projecting the artists' inner world, among others'.[6] The reader should bring this problem back into the context of what we said at the end of chapter five: the known elephant is not like the seen elephant! But the parallel is not quite as simple as that might suggest.

These are only hints, the primary purpose of which is to prevent you remaining within the grip of a naïve realism with regard to art and the discussion of art. Adequate understanding of art can be reached only within a larger methodological context than we have attempted to describe in this book, a context which would involve an appreciation of the unified complexity of man, of you. Moreover it involves engagement in some artistic modes. Nor, obviously, is such engagement enough. Dancing may be a regular occurrence in your life, but a selfattentive appreciation of such an art-form requires that performance be moved into the context of introspective methodology. Thus, 'the almost universal confusion of self-expression with dance-expression, personal emotion with balletic emotion, is easy enough to understand if one considers the involved relations that dance really has to feeling and its bodily symptoms'.[7] 'To keep virtual elements and actual materials separate is not easy for anyone without philosophic training . . . It takes precision of thought not to confuse an imagined feeling, or a precisely conceived emotion that is formulated in a perceptible symbol, with a feeling or emotion actually experienced in response to real events. Indeed, the very notion of feelings and emotions not really felt, but only imagined, is strange to most people.'[8]

[6] L. Lewisohn, *The Permanent Horizon*, 1934, 134.
[7] Langer, 1953, 183.
[8] Langer, 1953, 181.

With this quotation we have rather abruptly plunged the reader into a complex theory of art. Still, the plunge can be wholesome, bringing you perhaps to a particular realization of what we talked about in general in chapter one, a realization of the need for a refined type of reflection on all the patterns of experience of contemporary society if man is to get to grips with his own renewal. One might consider present orientation in dance forms in this light, recalling that 'the dance often reaches the zenith of its development in the primitive stage of a culture when other arts are just dawning on its ethnic horizon',[9] considering also the secularization of the dance,[10] its particular mode as virtual gesture of power, its relation to the problem mentioned by Lonergan of liberation of consciousness within the contemporary scene.

Let us return now from these hints and wider considerations to bring you to some notion of the underlying view of art. Need we recall here the story of the physicist and the lady?

We can state briefly then that art involves the objectification of a purely experiential pattern. Here let us tease out slowly what we mean by that. First of all, we will slip over the word 'pattern', assuming that the reader is familiar with it in its normal usage. The pattern in question here is experiential, auditory, visual, motor, etc. It is purely experiential, of the seen as seen, etc. One can best indeed understand 'purely' as qualifying the complex expression 'experiential pattern'. There is involved then both an exclusion and an inclusion. There is involved an exclusion of alien patterns and influences that instrumentalize experience. Such alien patterns and influences can be practical, scientific, philosophic or motivational. Most evident is the practical influence: then, for example, seeing red is instrumental to putting on the brake, hearing a bell may be instrumental to downing tools. Less evident is the motiva-

[9]Langer, 1953, ix.
[10]*Ibid.*, 187, 492 ff.

tional: one can go to an art exhibition and look long merely because it is the thing to do.

But the inclusion is the positive and important element here. The inclusion connotes that the seen is seen and the heard is heard with all its associations, spontaneously. One may note that this does not exclude a didactic component, but that component must have the quality of spontaneity, it must not be an imposed alien pattern. Again, the inclusion goes deeper. There is on the level of the psyche an orientation which, as it were, resonates with the orientation of man's intelligence that is expressed in questions, in wonder. With that orientation is associated feelings of awe, of the uncanny, fascination.[11] 'Purely experiential pattern' connotes a liberation of that orientation, a relief and an openness, an expansion along the lines of its own proper rhythm. We might recall here Charles Morgan's description of the function of dramatic art, extending its application to other forms of art: 'Dramatic art has a double function—first to still the preoccupied mind, to empty it of triviality, to make it receptive and meditative: then to impregnate it. Illusion is the impregnating power. It is that spiritual force in dramatic art which impregnates the silence of the spectator, enables him to become or perceive or imagine.'[12] There is a lifting of the person out of the ready-made world, a translation from the pressures of home and office, economics and politics, from the time of daily doing to the time of music, from the print and prose of news and science to language no longer instrument of literal meaning but pool of psychic possibilities. It is a withdrawal from practicality to an exploration of the possibilities of living in a richer world. Debussy put the point well when he remarked, writing to

[11]We might draw here on Rudolf Otto's little book, *The Idea of the Holy* (Penguin) but not of course on his deficient realism.
[12]See 'The Nature of Dramatic Illusion', in *Essays by Divers Hands,* edited by R. W. Macan, London 1933, 70.

Stravinsky, 'for me it is a special satisfaction to tell you how much you have enlarged the boundaries of the permissible in the empire of sound.'[13] One might say that, just as the mathematician explores possibilities relevant to science, so the artist explores the potentialities of total human living. All living involves artistry, is dramatic, but art focuses in its objectification of purely experiential patterns a possibility of fuller living, more integral meaning. Depending on the state of a culture, that objectification can be expressive of a rich common meaning and a common aspiration, or on the other hand it can include elements of 'shock', artistic isolation,[14] entombment in museums, liturgy without light or life.

We have said that art involves the objectification of a purely experiential pattern, but as yet we have not discussed objectification. In her later work Langer has a long discussion of the projection of feeling in art,[15] and we make no attempt to reproduce that treatment or its larger and essential context. But let us give some indications.

So far we have been dealing in a general way rather with what is projected and also received according to the responsiveness of the public.[16] It is within the context of this prior discussion that one might treat of the identity of known and knower, of seer and seen, etc. One talks of a work of art as being dynamic, alive, but it is you, the perceiver, the listener, that is alive and coming to life. But there is the transition from identity to expression involved in objectification which in many ways parallels the objectification which occurs on the level of intellect. Here we will emphasize, in a manner which should prove helpful, one parallel, by relating our treatment here of

[13]Quoted in Donald Mitchell's *The Language of Modern Music*, London 1966, 22.
[14]The little work by Donald Mitchell just cited illustrates this element of shock and isolation well, for example, in the case of Schoenberg.
[15]Langer, 1967, 4.
[16]Langer, 1953, 396 ff.

objectification to what we said in the preceding chapter about symbolic technique involving a certain objectification of mind. Before touching on that parallel we must recall what was already mentioned in our earlier quotations concerning the dance, that the expression in art is not spontaneous self-expression, it is 'emotion recollected in tranquillity'. There is involved a detachment of the artist from himself, the introduction of what might be called psychic distance. The objectification involves, too, a mediation of total mind, an appreciation of significance, an idealization of the purely experiential pattern. There is an unfolding, a revealing, of import, detached from the accidentals of concrete experience. But the detachment from accidentals is not an abstraction yielding formulation: the pattern cannot be conceptualized.

Now it is of great interest to note here that much of what we say has been said perhaps better and at greater length elsewhere. But saying and meaning are different things. What we mean, for example, by asserting the impossibility of conceptualization involves a context of introspective methodology. The meaning of conceptualization involves the meaning of intelligible emanations, of understanding and its expression, a meaning reached only insofar as one scientifically attends in one's own performance to the processes of insight and formulation and the transition from one to the other.

We may turn now to the question of a partial parallel between the last chapter and this by considering the following quotation:

In actual felt activity the form is elusive, for it collapses into a condensed and foreshortened memory almost as fast as the experience passes; to hold and contemplate it requires an image which can be held for contemplation. But there is no simple image of our inner dynamism as there is of visually perceived forms and colours and sound patterns. A symbol capable of articulating the forms of feeling is, therefore, necessarily presented in some sort of projection as an extra-organic structure that conveys the movement of emotive and perceptive processes. Such a projection is a work of art. It presents the semblance of feeling so directly to logical intuition that we seem to perceive feeling itself in the work; but of course the work does not contain feeling, any more than a proposition about the mortality of Socrates contains a philosopher.[17]

A preliminary remark recalls our warning earlier in this chapter about naïve realism. Langer points out at one stage that ' "space-tension" is an attribute belonging only to virtual space, where *esse est percipi*'.[18] This statement might usefully be considered here, and also linked with our remarks about the identity of known and knower, and objectification. The virtual space, the space of the picture, is no more out-there than real space is. In paradoxical and question-raising fashion we might add of course that it is, in a certain sense, more out-there: we leave the reader to sort that out. Again, whether one is reading sentences in a book of science or in a book of poetry, there is to be distinguished the print as seen and the real print. The real print is not *like* the seen print: the real print, as in the case of anything real, is to be known through correct understanding. Not that correctly understanding the nature of real print is the scientific reader's aim: the reader's aim is to understand what is meant, what is written about. The reader of the written work of art, however, is not operating in that intellectual pattern. He is orientated towards that total response that we have been describing. Because of this the print and the sound are not just media for the understanding of something, as they are for the scientific reader. They are responded to in ways we have been trying to indicate in this chapter.

[17]Langer, 1967, 67.
[18]Langer, 1953, 371.

At all events, it is insofar as you think within the context of structured critical realism that you will grasp correctly what is going on, what is meant in particular by the concluding sentence of the lengthy quotation above from Susanne Langer. And in that context you must stay if the parallel we make between symbolic logic and the art-logic is not to be misunderstood or understood mythically. Like symbolic logic, the art-work is a 'moving-object' for the human subject, but in a different pattern, a total pattern. Again, just as symbolic logic has developed in complexity and technique, embodying in apt symbolism the strategies of contemporary implication etc., so art and artistry develop in complexity and technique, embodying in apt 'extraorganic structures' the artistic import. But in contrast with symbolic logic, that 'extraorganic structure' is not merely an objectification of mind, but an objectification of man and his human possibilities. We leave the reader to exploit the parallels thus briefly indicated, to push them as far as they will go, to pick out their inadequacies. You could for a start return to the quotation from Langer which we have given and read it in reference to the previous chapter, replacing the word 'feeling' in it by the word 'thought'.

Furthermore, the parallels indicated are not restricted to symbolic logic. Besides the apt symbolism there is the calculating machine, besides logical systems there is technology. Moreover, the wider objectification of mind connoted here involves not merely logic but science, not merely science but philosophy and theology. For the wider objectification is not merely an objectification of logic or science, it is an objectification of man. It is an objectification of man for one thing because man must live largely within that objectification: it is his home, his city. Here perhaps the reader begins to see the link-up between technology and art, and the influence for better or worse of a philosophy or a theology on technology.

9

If man is a machine, all that is required is a greater machine in which he may fit as a cog. If man is conceived to any extent as a machine, there will be an ever-present tendency to fit him in as a cog. But man is not a machine. To treat here of the hierarchy of integrated aggregates and the unified levels of orientations that is man would be impossible. But common sense and art cling to what theory seeks to grasp: man does not take kindly to being considered a machine. Furthermore, not only is human intelligence and will beyond the mechanical: man's entire conscious life lies beyond the scope of any form of biological or neural determinism, and so there is the demand for liberation not only on the level of mind but on the level too of feeling.

We have been speaking of the evil effect and the inadequacies of wrong explanation. But neither is correct explanation, even when supplemented by practical common sense, adequate to human living: 'explanation does not give a man a home'.[19] There is needed not merely fire and shelter but a home and a hearth, not merely food for the mind and organs but for the psyche. Such are the needs of living, and their neglect within a culture can be mirrored in a failure within education for living. 'Artistic training is, therefore, the education of feeling, as our usual schooling in factual subjects, and logical skill such as mathematical "figuring" or simple argumentation (principles are hardly ever explained), is the education of thought. Few people realize that the real education of emotion is not the "conditioning" effected by social approval and disapproval, but the tacit, personal, illuminating contact with symbols of feeling. Art education, therefore, is neglected, left to chance, or regarded as a cultural veneer.'[20] But besides the education of the child there is the education and continued orientation of the adult, the education of a people. That education requires the

19Lonergan, *Insight*, 547.
20Langer, 1953, 401.

orientation and reach of artistry, and it has as many modes as the modes of artistry. We might survey briefly some of these modes, treated at length by Susanne Langer, especially in *Feeling and Form*.

There is the painting, which draws man out of the weary space of common life into a virtual space, a space which is not real, which is not measured by the steps of the fly walking on the canvas. There is music, song, and poetry, which open man to his history and his potentialities, which reveal to him through layers of resonances the meaning of his life, his people. There is the lyric, expressive of the individual subject, and the drama, expressive of the destiny of the group. One can think here not only of the more remote and refined symphony or opera, but of the ballad, the war-time songs, the immediately popular songs. It is in such regions that one may find the soul of a people, their common meaning. In this context one might consider, for example, daily and weekly papers and magazines with their offer of minimal meaning.

Then there is sculpture in general, which 'effects the objectification of self and environment for the sense of sight'.[21] There is the statue and there is architecture, and these are related to each other as the lyric and the drama. While the statue is a visual presentation of the space that feels which is man, architecture is expressive of the orientation of a people. 'The primary illusion of plastic art, *virtual space*, appears in architecture as *envisagement of an ethnic domain*.'[22] The reader should consider in this light, and in the context of critical realism for which the real is not just the seen, the objectification of human meaning which is the city. It is the product of meaning and meaninglessness, with street-names and structures echoing the existential memory and orientation of the people. That dialectic of meaning and meaninglessness may have left the city soulless,

[21]Langer, 1953, 91.
[22]Langer, 1953, 100; italics in text.

its heart the haunt of ad-men, pulsing with hasty movement, encompassed by beige suburban dullness. But the dialectic continues. To that dialectic the present chapter is a contribution. We may recall here the question of control of emergent meaning raised in chapter one. It is not the control of the ad-men or the machine, but of personal intelligence, a directiveness growing through the appreciation of the orientations of man, and of meaning in its emergence and expression. It is not for the methodologist or the theologian to trespass in the field of art or into human sciences. But 'inasmuch as he knows that the detached, disinterested, unrestricted desire to know is a key instance of the universal law that *omnia Deum appetunt*, he is in a position not only to encourage scientists to complete fidelity in their calling but also to teach non-scientists the high office of the scientific spirit; and in this fashion he can hope not only to promote scientific willingness to undertake fundamental research but also to mitigate the pressures that are exerted by so-called practicality and that ever seek to turn scientists away from their proper tasks and to direct their energies to projects with a significance, that because it is minimal, easily is understood.'[23] It is for the human scientist and the artist to raise up man and his city, so that his world may be a reaching towards heaven. It is for the theologian and the methodologist to appreciate and express the basic structure of that reaching, to point out in particular that 'art draws attention to the fact that the splendour of the world is a cipher, a revelation, an invitation, the presence of one who is not seen, touched, grasped, distinguished by a difference, yet present', that 'man is nature's priest and nature is God's silent communing with man'.[24]

[23]B. Lonergan, *Insight*, 746.
[24]These quotations are from the lecture on art given by Lonergan which we have already mentioned.

12

An End and a Beginning

WE began by telling the reader that the crucial issue was an experimental one, and throughout the book we have been returning to this fact. However, telling you that the issue is experimental is rather less than half the battle, for it is easy to say to yourself that the crucial issue is experimental and then pass swiftly on. It is easy enough to come to some understanding of the words, it is easy enough to memorize the key terms and so be able to manipulate them in the fashion that sometimes passes for understanding: for, it is both easy and common to turn away from your own nescience and hide it both from yourself and others with a cloak of rhetoric. In Karl Jaspers's terms it is easy to paraphrase the mystery and then take the paraphrase for an explanation.

Because this book is experimental it continually points away from itself to your own activities: 'if one desires to get beyond words and suppositions to meanings and facts, then one has to explore one's own mind and find out for oneself what there is to be meant; and until one does so, one is in the unhappy position of the blind man hearing about colours and the deaf man reading about counterpoint.'[1] Now the exploration of your own mind is not an easy task and to think that you have completed the enquiry because you have read this book would

[1] B. Lonergan, *Verbum: Word and Idea in Aquinas*, xii.

be to miss the point entirely. Of course very few readers will make the mistake of thinking that once they have read the book they have completed the task. Most will realize that there are other books to be read and may turn to the labour of reading them. But this may be just a more sophisticated way of missing the point. For, to understand your own understanding it is not sufficient to have read with care all the available books which purport to deal with the problem. When all the reading is done the crucial experiment, which you must do yourself and which no one can do for you, remains. This book is just a guide to that crucial experiment. It is not the experiment itself, but simply a series of printed hints on how to carry it out.

If you were already a master of your own understanding when you took up this book, if you already understood what it was to understand, then to understand our meaning was an easy task, it was merely a question of reading. But you may not be ready to assert that you already understood your own activity of understanding, and if this was the case then your task was immeasureably more difficult. For you must learn, and that in a peculiar mode of learning. You must use our book, our selected hints, as a guide to the appreciation of your own activities of intelligence. You must produce that data again and again, attend to it in the introspective mode, catching now and then a further glimmer of light. It is a slow and painful process. It is a long-term process that goes against the trend of a culture which clamours for instant information and of an educational tradition which increasingly, rather than guide the culture, succumbs to its demands. To undertake this task is to begin an intellectual conversion.

We have been concerned with an experiment but not just a searching, indeterminate experiment. We have not been content to claim that human understanding was a worthy object of study. We have suggested a method, a reflectively elaborated technique for the understanding of understanding. This method

we have called scientific introspection and we have been
engaged in trying to lead the reader to begin this introspecting.
Nonetheless, despite our persistent efforts, even this method
can become a superstition. There is the temptation to say that
because you have a method the solutions will come tumbling
out like the pennies from a slot machine, or the answers from a
computer. But this is a myth, for understanding and judgement
are not automatic and we cannot understand merely because
we want to.[2] This non-automatic character of inquiry and of
method accounts for some of the peculiarities of this book.

Our stress on the personal character of the experiment throws
some light on the nature of hand-books and schools of philosophy. What is on the page is print, marks, the conventional
expression of the formulation of the author's understanding.
If you reflect for a moment on your own expression you will
discover that understanding and expression are not the same
thing. Take as an example the term 'understanding'. Before you
read this book and attempted to perform the experiment suggested, you had heard the word 'understanding', and probably
you had used the word frequently enough. Now that you have
read the book and gone some way in the experiment you can
still use the word 'understanding' but what you mean now is,
perhaps, very different from what you meant before. In other
words the same term is used to express quite different meanings.
If your expression can remain constant through shifts of meaning, think how two different people may use identical expressions to mean quite different things. It is tempting to think that
identity of expression evidently indicates identity of meaning,
and to yield to that temptation is, in matters scientific, to open
the way to decadence, inauthenticity. Thus, for example, one
may preserve within a tradition the words of Aquinas without
the meaning uttered by the understanding of Aquinas.

Once again we indulge in the strategy of pulling the reader

[2]Cf. B. Lonergan, *Insight*, 525; *Verbum: Word and Idea in Aquinas*, 216.

up short. It is easy to acknowledge verbally the existence of this temptation, to keep the words and let the meaning slip away, to acknowledge the force of the temptation in others but not in yourself. We have found in our teaching that if the learner does not clearly catch himself in the act of yielding to this temptation, does not precisely appreciate himself turning to the book or the teacher for an answer in place of a turning to his own experience, or does not scientifically find himself tempted to rely on memory for the semblance of a solution, then he is missing the mark.

A school of philosophy can become something like a manual. It can become a club whose members gain confidence and warmth from the assurance that others think as they do. We do not say that a school must become like this; we merely note that it is a temptation. For, a school of philosophy is a group of people and, like every other group, it is subject to the pulls of group-interest. Further, the individual member does not want to be left out in the cold and so he inclines to follow the crowd, to echo their views, to remember when he does not understand. The immediate self-interest or protectiveness reinforces and is reinforced by the tendency to slip into the easy illusion that the answer is in the book. Against the dominance of handbook and school we have attempted to initiate in you a critical self-understanding, for

the philosopher's reasonableness is grounded on a personal commitment and on personal knowledge. For the issues in philosophy cannot be settled by looking up a handbook, by appealing to a set of experiments performed so painstakingly by so-and-so, by referring to a masterful presentation of overwhelming evidence in some famous work. Philosophic evidence is within the philosopher himself. It is his own inability to avoid experience, to renounce intelligence in inquiry, to desert reasonableness in reflection. It is his own detached, disinterested desire to know. It is his own advertence to the polymorphism of his own consciousness. It is his own insight into the manner in which insights accumulate in mathematics, in the empirical sciences, in the myriad instances of common sense. It is his own grasp of the dialectic unfolding of his own desire to know in its conflict with other desires that provides the key to his own philosophic development and reveals his own potentialities to adopt the stand of any of the traditional or new philosophic schools. Philosophy is the flowering of the individual's rational consciousness in its coming to know and take possession of itself. To that event, its traditional schools, its treatises, and its history are but contributions; and without that event they are stripped of real significance.[3]

There is an Arab proverb which has it that the way of truth is solitary and it is this fact that we have been in our fashion trying to elucidate. If a man wants to go on a journey he can be given a map, but he must make the journey himself.

The data of the philosopher are his own experiencing, his own inquiring and understanding, his own reflecting and judging, his own decisions and delights. But these activities occur in all men and all men are not philosophers. Philosophy begins when a man seriously asks himself what is going on within himself when he performs these activities. We have tried to get you to ask this question of yourself, and have given some directions towards a solution. Now such a question can be phrased in two ways: for example, What is understanding? and, What am I doing when I understand? Although both questions can be taken in the present context to mean the same thing, the second formula reveals explicitly what is implicit in the first. When one studies one's conscious acts, experiencing, inquiring and so on, by the method which we have tried to

[3]B. Lonergan, *Insight*, 429.

illustrate here, then 'one discovers not only the acts and their intentional terms but also the intending subject'.[4] As our experiment progressed not only did we try to lead you to a discovery of yourself as intending subject, but the intending subject became increasingly the focus of attention.

So we attempted to lead you to an understanding of yourself as source of meaning in science, in common sense, in art. Human society was revealed as the expression of a dialectic of meanings not unrelated to but still not determined by the lower levels.

At least since Søren Kierkegaard there has been in continental European philosophy a stress on the human subject. The attention has shifted from human nature to the person and his possibilities. With both Sartre and the late Maurice Merleau-Ponty this shift has been so great that they deny the validity of the notion of 'human nature'. Related to a concern for subjectivity, there are the common claims that our technological society is becoming increasingly inhuman, is swiftly becoming an environment in which the human person finds it more and more difficult to live and develop. For some the answer seems to be a retreat into a mythic golden age, a hankering after a past endowed with the advantages which our world so conspicuously lacks. But the past, whether mythic or real, like romantic Ireland, is with O'Leary in the grave. Such thoughts are anodynes, not solutions.

The modern world is one in that the economics of one state can affect the economics of another state over five thousand miles away, in that political changes and upheavals are rarely the exclusive concern of the country in which they occur, in that the advances in communications enable one to know to-day what, even in the last century, might have taken weeks to filter through. But the world is not one in meaning. In the one country there is no longer a common culture. The person

[4]B. Lonergan, *Verbum: Word and Idea in Aquinas*, ix.

grows up and asks what he is to become and finds a myriad suggestions and vying modes of seeking an answer. Into this confusion can come the totalitarian politician with his unique suggestions about what a person is to be and what society is to be like. He gains control over the communication system, over the economy, over the polity, and attempts to build an environment in which other suggestions will be suppressed, in which contrary insights will not occur. Whether he knows it or not, what he is trying to do is rigidly control human meaning. He is doomed to eventual failure, for men remain intelligent and insights will occur, but he can be relatively successful for a time and by constantly shifting his ground he can maintain control.

Amid the bedlam of conflicting meanings what is needed is not an authoritarian control of meaning, not a dictatorship nor a censor. What is needed is a method liberating man and his mind. Such we think is the significance of the present approach, for the method that will suffice to meet the demand cannot be something imposed from without with the possibility of becoming a dictatorship or a censorship. It is a method that will enable the human subject to come to a grasp of himself as source of meaning, thus facilitating not only his understanding of meaning but his judgement about meaning. Method, however, is not an end but a beginning. It is a beginning that is demanded.

Again, if method is not to become a mere superstition, is not to become a shallow verbal tradition, the aim of understanding must constantly be stressed. In the present context we emphasize that the problem of that stress is the person's own problem, your private problem. But however private that problem, the fruits of facing it, however small, will be manifest. The unremitting effort at self-understanding will gradually build up a mediation of your own and others' meaning. The mediation of meaning is something like a developing appreciation of music. Take the man who rarely listens to music and considers it a jumble of noise when he does. He might one day say to himself that perhaps those who find some meaning in this jumble are right, and so he sits down to listen. Ever so slowly he may move to the beginnings of an appreciation which, if he continues his effort, continually develops and in some way transforms his living. He has become a new person. But note that it is he and not the music that has changed. In somewhat the same way, as you move to an ever more delicate understanding of yourself, as your discovery of yourself as intending subject becomes more profound, you will grow in an appreciation of ranges of human meaning, your living will be changed through the intellectual conversion.

We have been discovering the human person as a project, as an unending movement which can be either progress or decline, development or decay. We have discovered in a preliminary way the mode of development and the manner of the decline. But if the human person is a project, if you are a developing thing directing your own development, that growth remains both into the unknown and precarious. It is precarious, for at no time can you claim that your position is secure; what you have built up may in some way fall and shatter. It is into the unknown because at your present stage you perhaps appreciate the next step, but you have no clear idea of the possibilities that may open up. You may see to the next ridge but until you have gained the ridge you do not see beyond. There is the unknown, there is the precarious, there is basic sin: and here the human subject finds himself oriented to mystery, reaching out and up to mystery. Nor are intimations of that mystery lacking, for we are living in a world that is redeemed and in which a certain revelation has taken place. And so the human subject is a reaching out to the Three Persons in whom finally he hopes his mind and his will, he himself, will eventually come to rest.

With the realization of that revelation comes the demand with which you are now familiar, the desire to understand. The science of theology is the fruit of that desire to understand turning to revelation. Theology is the effort to understand the mystery which, paradoxically, rather than resolve it, only reveals more fully its mysteriousness. We recall here the theory of inverse insight, but now the hindrance is, not lack, but super-abundance of intelligibility. Theology is the science which in this life ends with Aquinas's assertion that of God we know nothing but that he exists. But it is too the science that reveals most clearly the boundless desire of man to understand, that reveals the basic and inescapable orientation of man, and not of man in general but of each person, to mystery. It reveals, in the context of faith, the ulterior reach of the human subject to untrammelled vision. But, far from turning away from society and leaving it to its own devices, the theologian turns to encourage man in the making of man, to win for his science the respect due to it as a fulfilment of the pure desire to know and as a component in that making, to point out to society that if it is to be an adequate context for men it must continually avoid the tendency to stifle that desire with demands which, because they are immediately practical, are appealing, but in the end detrimental and destructive even of the practicality they are called on to support.

Such is the project. This chapter is an end in the obvious sense that it is the last one and that the book is completed. But it is a beginning in the only sense that has real significance. For it marks the beginning of an operation, an investigation, the nature of which even the diligent reader may have misconceived, even until now. If so, there is the chance of a new beginning insofar as a reader may suspect some one point of divergence between our meaning and his or hers. At all events, we end as we began: the crucial issue is experimental, and the experiment is yours.

Problem 1.

HOCUS
POCUS

PRESTO

This is not a particularly difficult problem and, indeed, to find its solution is a pretty routine job. What we are interested in doing is getting you to appreciate the difference between solving the problem and self-attending to the process of solution in scientific fashion. Any schoolboy may approach the problem in the first manner: the second approach carries one into methodology.

We have already given various indications of the differences between the approaches. Here the reader will find further hints. One point, for instance, is to note what the data for the problem are. Strictly speaking your data for this problem are black marks on the page. Anything beyond the black marks is your contribution. On the other hand of course the central data for methodology is your own wonder in its engagement with the problem. Most of the statements to follow are calculated to turn attention to that data: they are, if you like, metadescriptive.

Because you know the English language and are able to read you begin to specify the problem. To begin with you realize that it is a problem. You then, we hope, make a further and necessary assumption. You appreciate the insignificance of the fact that the letters form three words. You assume that the letters make a sum. Again, you call on your background knowledge of the series 0, 1, 2, 3, 4, 6, 7, 8, 9, and the rules of multiplication, addition, and so on. If you did not have this background the problem would be impossible.

Having understood what the problem might be, that is, having not only an experience but having asked a question from a prior context of understanding, you set down to the business of finding a solution. Is the sum addition, multiplication or subtraction? How do you know? Having settled that it is an addition sum, you ask what values could be assigned. At this stage we note that in these problems, while the reader should pause to puzzle, to solve, the text runs on.

A certain amount of reflection might suggest that the leading letter, P, must be equal to 1. But note that such a suggestion will rest on certain spontaneous assumptions: after all, no indication was given that the letters had values less than ten, nor indeed that the decimal system was being used. Following up this opening you consider the sum $H+1=1R$.

Since the sum $H+1$ goes into two figures you might quickly conclude that $H=9$. But is it? After all, the two o's in the fourth place of the sum, despite appearances, do not mean zeros: so a unit may be carried. So perhaps $H=8$? You find yourself driven to seeking light by returning both to the data and to already acquired results. Even if $H=9$, R cannot be greater than 1. But P is already equal to 1. On the assumption that different letters have different values, R will have to be zero. But what about H? You might let your native wonder rest in this region of the data for a spell.

Perhaps another region would yield up insight. Consider the letter S. Certain values are excluded at once, namely, zero and 1. 5 too can be eliminated, since $5+5=$ten, which would make the letter o equal to zero, and this cannot be, since we already have R equal to zero. You may push on thus to consider the possibility of excluding other values, to arrive at a definite value for S.

The temptation to get interested only in doing the sum may become great and so one should continually break to reflect on the process. All along we are expressing possible movements of intelligence. Your task, never forget, is to advert to these movements, or similar insights you may have in trying to solve the problem independently. Notice how you have moved from merely looking at the letters to making or taking suggestions about possible relations between numbers. Nor are you satisfied at any stage with mere suggestions, with possibilities: you want to know if the suggestions are correct, if your hunch would work out, and so you check your own or our suggestions. In the words now familiar to you, you are constantly moving from experience to understanding to judgement —nor are attitudes of will irrelevant. You will, of course, catch yourself regularly asking the two basic questions which we pointed out were the hinges of the movement, the What–question and the Is–question: what is the value of P?; it would seem to be 1, but is it so?

It is important to notice that the oscillation from experience to understanding and judgement is both spontaneous and frequent: this is related to the common difficulty of finding the basic structure verified in so-called immediate judgements. You do not have to be told that the result must be checked at each stage. As you go along you check the suggestions you have already made and so you can say after each step that this much must be so.

Let us return to the sum. The values zero, 1, and 5, are excluded for S. But 2 is possible. So try 2. When you insert 2, the following values are assigned:

$$
\begin{array}{r}
9\ 4\ C\ U\ 2 \\
1\ 4\ C\ U\ 2 \\
\hline
1\ \varnothing\ 8\ 2\ T\ 4\ \ [\varnothing = \text{zero}]
\end{array}
$$

So far so good. But when you go further the snags appear. C+C= 2, which means that C must equal either 1 or 6. C cannot equal 1 since P is equal to 1, so it must equal 6. But if C=6, then 1 is carried to the next column and 0+0 [now assigned the value 4+4] will equal 9 and not 8. But if the E equals 9, then H cannot equal 9, which, unless 1 is carried, it must. But 1 is not carried: so the suggested value for S turns out to be unacceptable. S cannot equal 2.

The other possibilities can be tried out in the same way. We will not go into them here. What is important for the reader as he goes on with the problem is that he constantly returns to himself in the act of this intelligent juggling.

Problem 2.

A man was given twelve marbles and a balance. The marbles appeared to be identical but he was told that one marble was of a different weight from all the others. By weighing the marbles against one another in the balance not more than three times he was able to discover the odd marble and tell if it was heavier or lighter than the others. How did he do it?

Once again our interest is in catching ourselves intelligently working at the problem in order to initiate ourselves into scientific introspection.

Your first inclination might be to divide the marbles into two groups of six and weigh one group against the other. This would be wasteful. Why? What would you learn by doing this? That one group was heavier than the other group? But you already know this before weighing since the odd marble is in one of the groups. You would learn which was the heavier of the two groups. But would this do you any good? You have wasted one turn on the balance and you still have twelve marbles to weigh.

So you look around for other groupings. Say, three groups of four or four groups of three. Three groups of four seems better since you weigh eight marbles instead of six on the first weighing. Let us work that out.

Call the three groups AAAA, BBBB and CCCC. Weigh group AAAA against group BBBB. There are two possible outcomes: either group AAAA=group BBBB or it does not.

If AAAA=BBBB then the odd marble must be in CCCC and must be found in the next two weighings. Let us assume this is the case. What do you do next? What have you learned by the first weighing? That the odd marble is in group CCCC. Is that all? Haven't you also learned that all the marbles in groups AAAA and BBBB are of equal weight? Can this information be used? Perhaps some marbles from the first two groups might be used as checks. What about weighing two marbles from AAAA against two from CCCC? AA against CC: what would you learn from this? If AA= CC then the odd marble would be one of the other two from CCCC and you would have only one chance left to discover which one of the two it was and whether it was lighter or heavier. It would be

10

quite easy to discover which marble was the odd one, but you have no guarantee that you will discover its relative weight. So AA against CC is a blind alley.

Try another arrangement. What about using only one guide marble A and three unknown marbles from CCCC in the arrangement AC against CC? If AC=CC then the remaining marble is the odd one and its weight can be easily discovered in the next weighing. But what if AC does not equal CC? What do you learn in this case? That the uneven marble is one of the C marbles on the balance. Certainly, you learn that. But is that all? Don't you also learn which of the two groupings is heavier and which is lighter? Let us take it that group AC weighs down and is therefore the heavier of the two groupings. What do we know then about the marbles? Well, A is a guide marble and cannot be the odd one. C may be the odd marble and if it is then it is heavier than the other eleven marbles. For clarity call this marble C′. But either of the other two C marbles might be the uneven marble. If that was the case then the odd marble would be lighter than the other eleven. Call these marbles C° and C°°.

You have one weighing left to decide between C′, C°, and C°°. How are the marbles to be arranged? Do you have to put all three on the balance? Here we keep asking you questions relating to the problem: but you should continually recall that your central question throughout is, What am I doing? Notice, for instance, how we have selected an apt symbolism: do you find it apt enough?

Leave C° off the balance. What do you know about C°? That it might be the odd marble. Only that? No, you also know that if it is the odd marble it is lighter than the others. How will you discover if it is the odd one? If the groups that you do weigh against one another are equal. You are left with two marbles, C′ and C°°. What is known about them? If C′ is the odd marble it is heavier; if C°° is the odd marble it is lighter.

What arrangement is required to discover which is the odd marble if either of them is? What about weighing C′C°° against AA? If C′C°° equals AA, then C° is the odd marble and is lighter than the other eleven, as we saw. But what if C′C°° does not equal AA? Well, either C′C°° is heavier than AA or it is lighter than AA.

If C'C°° is heavier, then C' is the odd marble and is heavier than the other eleven. If C'C°° is lighter than AA, then C°° is the odd marble and is lighter than the other eleven.

So that is one half of the puzzle solved. Of course, if AAAA does not equal BBBB in the first place, then the odd marble is a member of either the group AAAA ot the group BBBB and another weighing arrangement has to be worked out. But we leave this part of the puzzle to the reader. There are enough clues in the foregoing to make the discovery of the remainder of the solution relatively easy.

In this puzzle you have come to appreciate somewhat, we hope, the process of accumulating insight: getting all the possible information at each stage and moving forward in its context. You will discover in your efforts to solve the remainder that if you let any piece of information slip by you, you will be unable to find the answer. You are trying to discover all the relations between the pieces, you are trying to amass all the clues. You may have found the solution somewhat difficult to follow on the page. You may have got muddled with AAAA, BBBB, C', C° and so on. And when you turn to do the rest of the puzzle you may be inclined to draw little marbles, or you may, as we did when we came across the problem first, actually get marbles or coins or such like. In other words, you try to provide for yourself an image that will help you get the sequence of insights. Spontaneously you do this, trying to set up the problem in such a way that insight might be evoked. Your task here is to appreciate that spontaneity, its source, its significance, its processes.

Again, if you have been following our solution to the problem intelligently and self-attentively you will have noticed yourself constantly asking the reflective question, Is it so? At each turn you were, we hope, rightly critical and self-attentive in that criticism: careful to make sure that we were proceeding correctly and also appreciative of the mental stance involved in that care. It was not of course a matter of merely understanding our words: you were trying to understand the problem, the clues, the solution; you were trying to grasp the correctness of each component in the solution; you were above all trying to appreciate the fluctuations of your wonder throughout.

Problem 3.

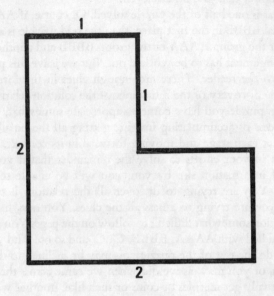

Divide the figure into
four identical parts.

First note that, unless your eyesight is poor, you have no difficulty
in seeing the figure. To see the figure you have merely to look. But
looking at the figure is no problem and does not pose a problem.
The problem arises when, besides looking, you ask a question, or
someone asks you a question. Here the question about the figure is,
How can it be divided into four equal parts? By the asking of the
question the figure has been raised from being the object of seeing
merely, to being now the object of inquiry.

How do you go about trying to solve the problem? Be very concrete. Don't try to remember what someone may have told you; don't try and recall what is said in this book. Just try to catch yourself in the act of trying to find a solution and question that activity. What in fact do you do? Perhaps you pick up a pencil and begin to draw in lines. Why are you doing this? Isn't it so that the solution, you hope, will almost spring out at you? Aren't you trying to manipulate the figure so that you may more easily get the solution? Why are you doing this? Did someone teach you to do it? Or is it spontaneous? We have sometimes referred to this activity as disposing the phantasm.

How have you tried to divide the figure? Have you tried squares rectangles, triangles? Have you had to throw these aside because they didn't work? Because they didn't satisfy your demand for explanation? What is your next move? Maybe you think about the data again. What are you given? An L-shaped figure. Is that all? What do you know about the dimensions of the figure? Is this relevant? Have you been using this piece of information? Or have you been overlooking this clue?

The figures you have been trying to make inside the main figure have, perhaps, all had their bases on the base lines of the main figure. Or were you always joining corners to make triangles? Why have you done this? Or can you really pin down a reason for any of your moves? Maybe the figures could start from the middle of the main figure? Anyhow, some more ambitious juggling with the figure is needed. Other shapes have to be tried. Perhaps the shape of the figure itself is a clue?

What you should try to appreciate in yourself when doing this problem is the way your intelligence permeates your fiddling about with the L-shape. You are not merely aimlessly but hopefully fiddling. Your efforts lie within the context of your habitual understanding and your juggling is oriented towards a particular inclement of understanding. In this orientation your intelligence is, as it were, ready to leap on any clue, examine any configuration insofar as it offers hope of solution, reject those whose unsuitability is grasped, etc.

Not only does this little example help you to appreciate what 'illuminate the phantasm' or 'dispose the phantasm' could mean, but it can help you—insofar as the solution was not evident or easy—to appreciate the involvement of the whole person. Not only was there the oscillation up and down from experience to judgement, but there was concern, perhaps frustration, irritation. And to solve the problem, fidelity to the intellectual pattern of experience, discussed in chapter six of *Insight*, was required.

Let us conclude this problem with another of the same type.

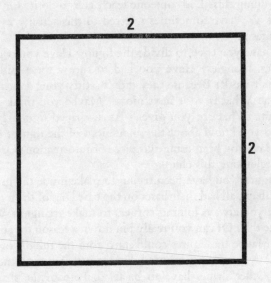

Divide the figure into
five identical parts.

You may well catch on immediately to our trick. But if you don't, if you catch yourself beginning to try various squares or shapes within the square, then you can appreciate how you have been 'conditioned' by the orientation of the previous problem. 'Conditioning' of course, can have the dimensions of any of the biases discussed in chapters six and seven of *Insight*.

Problem 4.

> Barn Burning
> Dry September
> Beyond
> Black Music
> Red Leaves
> The Middle Ground

This problem is an attempt to experiment against the background of our discussion of symbolic meaning in chapter eleven.

When you read over the lines it is unlikely that your response is one of complete incomprehension. At least the individual words are familiar and, further, at least each line is grammatical, although not a sentence. When you read all the lines you are not left with an entirely meaningless mental jumble. But the important question here is, Are you left with a mood, a mood which, even, if it is hard to specify, at least is quite different from the mood which is communicated by the evening paper?

Try now assorting the building blocks and see what happens:

> Black Music
> The Middle Ground
> Beyond Red Leaves
> Dry September
> Barn Burning

Is there a subtle difference of tone, which would be difficult to express? Again, what happens when one of the blocks is omitted, as follows:

> Black Music
> The Middle Ground
> Beyond
> Red Leaves
> Dry September

Various combinations of the blocks are possible, each combination yielding a slightly different mood, or rather evoking a slightly different response. It is one of the tasks of the critic to investigate the Why and the How of the evoking of such different moods and responses.[1] Such criticism, of course, can be mediated by a range of sciences, and it can take on the dimensions of an exegesis of symbolic meaning or of an investigation of the cultural or universal *a priori* of man's psyche. Our point for the moment, however, is to ask you to concentrate on the kind of meaning or response that was achieved in you. The poem is made of several blocks of images and the total effect is achieved not merely by the fact that there are five or six images, but by relative positioning. You may ask yourself, for example, whether your spontaneous reaction was to attempt to decipher the poem as if it were a telegram in code, or whether you allowed the images to 'wash over you'. And so on.

In this poem we have taken the liberty of moving the image blocks around, while keeping the word-groups together. This, obviously, was an arbitrary factor. The poem, in fact, was composed in a curious manner. Each word-group is the title of one of the short stories of William Faulkner. We went through the titles and picked out some that appealed to us. Then we played around with these and came up with the poem. Of course we do not claim that such poems are of any great value, but here their artistic value is not the issue. What we are interested in doing is illustrating the kind of

---

[1]While we discussed artistry in chapter eleven we passed over the questions of criticism and censorship. Perhaps the following indication would be helpful: ' . . . the exigence for formulation and abstract conceptual expression appears in the field of art. Not necessarily in the artist himself, who will sometimes decline to formulate the meaning of his work, but in the work of critics. What are the critics doing if not attempting to detach the meaning of the artistic creation from the particular image or form in which it is embodied or incarnate and universalize it, make it public intellectual property through words and concepts? However much the artist may contemn the critics as parasites on his creativity, it seems clear that the human race is not going to dispense with them; they answer to a basic need of the human cognitional structure. Finally, the exigence for truth is implicit in the moral judgement of the artist, when he asks, not whether his work has value as art, but what the morality is of his executing the work and presenting it to the public, *this* public in a particular state of development, education, etc. I think that, despite all their rebellion against the less intelligent elements in law and censorship, responsible artists do experience and submit to this exigence.' F. E. Crowe S.J., 'Neither Jew nor Greek, but one Human Nature and Operation in All', *Philippine Studies* (13) 1965, 560.

meaning that occurs when you read poetry. The reader may object that our procedure was entirely arbitrary. But was it? We selected the titles out of a long list, and we arranged the groups. Our selection and arranging was not governed by cold logic. We do not dispute that an entirely random procedure might have produced the same result, but this is no more interesting than the monkey typing the dictionary by chance. It is worth pointing out, then, that images and artistry are not the exclusive property of the artist: else, indeed, he would have no audience. The question of convention, too, is worth a thought. Take the pair of words, Black Music. The poet exploits the conventional significance and tone of the word-pair in his selection and juxtapositioning. The juxtapositioning is not merely local: it is a modification, an enlargement, a merging of significance. But evidently if convention is entirely ignored or unknown then there will not even be a communication of rhythm. Again, there is the fluid fringe of convention. What is our meaning—where by meaning is now meant the symbolic dimension, artistic response— of the word-group The Middle Ground? Does it overlap with yours? Would it be possible to discover whether it did or not?

I who have not sown,
I too,
By God's grace may come to harvest
And proud,
As the bowed
Reapers
At the Assumption
Murmur thanksgiving.

Patrick Kavanagh's *I May Reap*